Ojibwa Myths and Legends

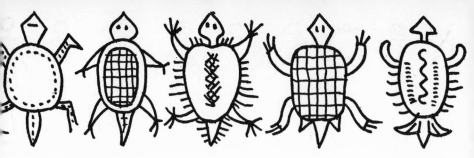

Ojibwa Myths

**Drawings by
Ruth Maney**

Ross and Haines, Inc., Publishers

And Legends

Sister Bernard Coleman

Ellen Frogner

Estelle Eich

Minneapolis, Minnesota, 1971

L.C. # 62-4096
ISBN #0-87018-010-X

DEDICATION

To our Ojibwa storytellers without whose contribution this book would not have been possible. May their tales become part of the great heritage of American folklore, and may their ancient lore be saved for their posterity.

TABLE OF CONTENTS

TABLE OF CONTENTS (continued)

TABLE OF CONTENTS (continued)

FOREWORD

Ojibwa Myths and Legends was prompted by two desires—to determine the status of story telling among the northern Minnesota Ojibwa of the mid-twentieth century and then granted that a substantial oral tradition should still exist, to make the myths and tales easily available. The response that came when we asked for narratives soon gave us an answer to our question concerning the status of story telling. The art is still alive, but only among the older Ojibwa. Our second desire—to make a significant regional literature easily available—grew stronger as we realized how fragile the oral tradition of the Minnesota Ojibwa is at the present time and how meager the number of recorded sources. The records that do exist are largely buried in scientific reports inaccessible to many readers.

The stories in *Ojibwa Myths and Legends* express aboriginal social and religious beliefs and an aboriginal economy. In these respects, they express the distinctive contributions of the Indian material in the total body of North American folk literature. The stories also reflect the interests and concerns that can be found in folk literature throughout the world and thus they attain a universality. All this we found at our very door, but the time for such finding is at an edge, and therefore a mid-twentieth century record has special significance.

For the knowledge that the older Ojibwa transmitted to us and for the graciousness with which they shared their background, we are indeed grateful. We are also grateful for the grant received from the University of Minnesota Fund for Regional Writing.

Sister Bernard Coleman
Ellen Frogner
Estelle Eich

CHAPTER ONE

STORY TELLING AMONG THE OJIBWA

AUGUST MORNINGS in northern Minnesota are often crisp reminders that summer will eventually be replaced by the season of frost and snow. It was on one of these mornings that we sat under the boughs of a tall spruce listening to the granddaughter of Chief Hole-in-the-Day relate tales and lore once told in her family's wigwam. A small number of friendly chickens walked around our chairs, a dog slept at our feet, and small children, as absorbed in their great aunt's stories as we were, sat nearby in the swing or on the ground. The narrator's face lit up with pleasure when she related incident after incident that happened during the time that "Nanabozho walked the earth," and she laughed outright when she placed Nanabozho in a modern setting. Then as she delved into history, she reminded us of the time when her people— the Ojibwa—were the principal inhabitants of the land surrounding the source of the Mississippi River. She wanted to be sure that we understood the facts about her grandfather as they had been interpreted to her, and so she recounted details of how Chief Hole-in-the-Day met his death at the hands of the Pillagers (the Leech Lake Ojibwa).

Our narrator went on to talk about her own childhood days. She recalled how as a youngster, she was sent away from home for three years to attend a school for Indian children. While there, she learned to speak English, but she did not give up her native tongue even though she was shamed for using it. Hers was a common experience, for other Ojibwa now in their sixties and seventies also told us about the problem of retaining their Indian language against the wishes of the white teachers.

The granddaughter of Chief Hole-in-the-Day is typical of a number of generous and talented Indian story tellers whom we met during the closing years of the 1950's, when under bright summer skies or in the cutting winds of late autumn, we made trip after trip to the northern Minnesota reservations in our search for traditional stories by the Ojibwa.[1] We went back to some of the narrators two or three times, or still more often. We believe that this is a good procedure. Making known our quest at

---

[1]There are eight of these Ojibwa reservations—Fond du Lac, Mille Lacs, White Earth, Leech Lake, Red Lake, Nett Lake Grand Portage, and Vermilion.

the first meeting was sometimes difficult, but after that, we were likely to be identified as the people who "wanted the real old stories." Fortunately several of the narrators felt at home with us immediately, for they had been known by one of the collaborators over a period of twenty-five years. With these people, it was possible to talk about members of the family, about changes on the reservation, or about a pet crow or a pet fawn. With new acquaintances, the mention of a character or an incident in a story or the use of an Ojibwa term often led into the telling of a whole tale. We each made our own record as we listened, and therefore in our research we had three independent reports for every narrative.

With two exceptions, the story tellers and informants (forty-four altogether) were older men and women between sixty-five and ninety-seven years of age. Twenty were women and twenty-four were men. In the total number, there were seventeen narrators who were particularly outstanding. The stories that they told are artistically complete, and authentic when compared with published material and the known traditions of the Ojibwa.

Most of the Ojibwa we interviewed seemed to be very conscious of historical events within the span of their own lives and the lives of their parents and grandparents. Some harbored old feelings of enmity based on claims to hereditary chieftainship, and more than once we heard extreme statements of dislike for the Sioux, with whom the Ojibwa fought for the wild rice lakes of northern Minnesota. Several commented on conflicts with the white people. They described the Leech Lake uprising of 1898, and many spoke of Chief Hole-in-the-Day and the chief's son. Others commented on the important treaties of 1854 and 1889, which were signed by members of families represented in our group of story tellers. Whether or not an acquaintance's name appeared on a particular treaty roll was a matter of great interest.

We heard comparatively little about the broader sweep of Indian history, although many of the old-time Ojibwa liked to use the term *An-ish-in-aub-ag,* meaning the early people. The term signifies a remote period in the history of the Ojibwa. It is also used to refer to other Algonquian Indians. Some of our Ojibwa narrators commented on how the early people living in the east along the St. Lawrence River came in conflict with the aggressive Iroquois and gradually migrated westward into the Great Lakes region.

At present, the older Ojibwa seem to feel that they are the last link with a distinctly Indian past. They recognize the fact that those who can relate the native traditions with sureness and relative completeness are rapidly becoming few in number. Story telling as an art and a custom is now at time's edge among the Ojibwa, quite in contrast to the set rules formerly maintained and the high esteem in which the art was once held. It used to be true that some of the narratives were considered sacred and so could be told only by certain individuals. There was also a designated time for story telling and in this respect the Ojibwa, like many other North American Indians, regarded winter as the only appropriate season. When the blustery winds blew against the stiff branches of the trees and piled the snow high on the trails, then young and old gathered in the warmth of the wigwam fire to listen to Ojibwa lore.

We asked our informants about the practice of reserving

4

story telling for the winter months. Some gave reasons related to the Ojibwa environment and economy. There was more time during the long cold winters and a need for a diversion. However, the reason that seemed uppermost in the mind of the old Ojibwa was the strong traditional belief that if stories were told in the summer, the animal manidos (or spirit beings) would then hear themselves spoken of. Frogs, toads, and snakes were feared particularly. Two of our informants—one at Fond du Lac and the other on the Leech Lake Reservation—reminded us that the frog or toad was no ordinary one. It was a tremendously big toad or a giant frog that would come out of the pond at night and pursue the narrator. Snakes may have been held in awe because of association with the mythological theme of the continuous warfare between the giant snakes and the Ojibwa culture hero, Nanabozho.

Some of the older Indians described for us scenes from their younger days when story telling was a part of everyday life. The first picture that follows takes us back to the time of the wigwam when the story teller was held in much esteem. Often an older member of the family—particularly a grandparent—was the narrator, but there was also in almost every camp or village, a man or woman especially talented in the telling of stories and perhaps in dramatizing an occasional scene. This person was identified as virtually a professional. Such a story teller appears now in the account given in the words of Brave Lady, who has lived all her life on the Leech Lake Reservation:

"When I was a real Indian and lived in a wigwam, we used to invite this old woman to come over in the evening to tell stories. We never grew tired of listening to her. I

5

can still see her standing before the fire acting out her stories. I remember how the flames danced up and down and made strange pictures on the inside of the wigwam. She told the same stories many times over, but each time we enjoyed them as much as before. Sometimes we listened until late in the night, or even until early morning. Some of these stories lasted for a whole winter."

The birchbark wigwam gradually gave way to the one-room log cabin and the small frame house, but this change in kind of dwelling had little effect on the customs of story telling. The Ojibwa clung tenaciously to their old myths and tales and the usual time for relating them. The first snowflake was still the sign that story telling time had arrived.

An eighty-year-old Ojibwa described for us story telling in his log cabin home on the White Earth Reservation in the 1880's. His account reflects social and economic history:

The men who had come to spend the evening had settled at White Earth through encouragement from a government offer of log cabins, stoves, cattle, and tools. They had left their homes on other reservations to join a caravan of over-loaded ox-carts that moved slowly over the deeply rutted trails, to arrive at last at their new homesite, White Earth. Now gathered together, they talked about the traditional patterns of barter, which were more or less easy going and quite in contrast to the white man's more definite techniques of bargaining. Our narrator explained what it meant to the Indian to change from an economy of hunting and fishing to one based on agriculture. This new way of making a living the govern-

6

ment pressed on them without full realization of the impact.

As the years went along, the same men continued to gather in the home of our informant. Now the men talked about the sorghum mill built by the government. They discussed the methods of the agricultural teachers who had been sent to demonstrate how to raise crops of wheat and oats. They laughed when they told how John Windigo, one of their own men, could plow a furrow straighter than that plowed by the government teacher. The men enjoyed telling tales of their prowess in encounters with caribou, deer, moose, bears, and buffalo. Then before the close of the evening, they resorted to the old Ojibwa tales of Nanabozho and his exploits.

A former Indian teacher of the village of Ponsford on the White Earth Reservation gave still another setting for an evening of story telling as she remembered it to be at about 1900:

"In the winter evenings we would gather at the home of an old woman story teller. When we arrived, we handed our contributions for the pot-luck lunch to the old woman, and settled down to talk about personal happenings and current tribal problems. A special concern was the education of our children outside the home, for this meant the breaking of family ties. Gradually the atmosphere changed from the serious to the jovial when our old friend began to relate incident after incident about the tricks of Nana-bozho. The evening closed with the pot-luck lunch of boiled porcupine, rabbit or deer meat."

The change from the wigwam to the log cabin or the small frame house did not occur at the same pace every-

7

where among the Ojibwa of northern Minnesota. Some Indians preferred to keep the traditional kind of dwelling. (Even in the late 1950's we found a few families using a wigwam during the summer.) Other Ojibwa were too remote to be much affected by the white man's customs in housing or shelter. However, no matter what kind of dwelling, one culture pattern that contributed to the solidarity of the family was the universal appeal of story telling.

One of our youngest narrators (born in 1903) on the Nett Lake Reservation came from a family who still lived in a wigwam in the early twentieth century. It was a family that represented the meeting of two cultures. The Ojibwa mother, competent in such traditional skills as harvesting and winnowing the wild rice, could not speak English; her husband, of Irish descent, could not speak Ojibwa. The mother was eager for her children to be educated in the traditions of both the Ojibwa and the white man. The children often read aloud selections from their school books, and the mother never tired of listening, especially if it happened to be her most highly treasured story, "Cinderella." At other times, the mother gathered the children around her and related old Ojibwa tales. There were several favorites, but one that our informant mentioned particularly was "The Rolling Head." No matter how many times the children listened to the story, the plight of the two brothers was always an occasion for a few tears or at least a great seriousness. But when the evil magician's moccasins were burned, then there was laughter in the wigwam.

"The Rolling Head" is one of the more than forty narratives contained in this volume. We heard three versions of the story; we have included two. In general, we have presented additional versions whenever there seems to be a special contribution, but not otherwise.

Some of the stories the Ojibwa tell are humorous; others are serious and at times tragic. The humor lies in absurd situations, roughness and vulgarity, and frequently a jovial kind of poetic justice. The serious or tragic appears in themes of cruelty, infidelity, death, misfortune, and the struggle for a livelihood. The narratives reflect the Ojibwa way of life, illustrating the fact that folk literature should not be separated from other aspects of a culture. Throughout the book, we have tried to make clear this vital relationship.

The classification of our material illustrates important aspects of Ojibwa folk literature. Part One includes such various types of narratives as fairy tales bearing resemblances to the European tradition, stories of Old Turtle, accounts of spirit wanderers and little people. Part Two concentrates on the stories about Nanabozho, the central character in Ojibwa folk literature. Part Three combines narrative and expository material in sections entitled "Notes on the Thunderbird" and "Nature Lore, Magic Practices, and Omens."

PART I

"ONCE UPON A TIME" STORIES

ONCE UPON a time" suggests that the story may be about a king, a prince, or a lovely princess. Hearing elderly Ojibwa tell stories of this type made us especially aware of the meeting of Indian and European ways.

The six narratives in the group of "Once upon a time" stories differ in the extent to which native material is used. At one extreme, there is "The Little Boy and the Windigo!" (It may even be that a story like this is Indian in origin, even though it has its counterparts elsewhere.) At the other extreme are the four narratives where Indian life penetrates very little or not at all: "The Rescue of the

11

Lovely Princess," "The Ogema's Son," "O, Marie," and "Linda." In between stands "The Homely One," as the introduction to the story explains.

*   *   *   *

THE HOMELY ONE

Here is one of the world's favorite plots. The unwanted or "least likely" girl (a Cinderella) through human or magical assistance marries happily after all, in spite of the unkindness of those around her.

True to Ojibwa tradition, it is the grandmother who is loyal to the girl and helps her. Details such as the wigwam, the ogema or chief, and the tumpline (a deerskin harness worn across the forehead and back over the shoulders) also reflect native life. Most significant is the fact that the courtship test—the main problem in the story—is in accordance with an Ojibwa custom. Parents used to require that the young people who were to be married demonstrate their ability to work hard and well. A young man had to go out hunting and return with meat for the girl's family. A young girl had to show her ability to bring in wood, make nets, or weave mats and baskets.

As a whole, the story that follows achieves a masterful unity of cultural setting and age-old plot.

*   *   *   *

Once upon a time there lived a chief or an ogema who had one son. The old chief thought, 'It's time I find a wife for my son."

The chief sent out word that all the young women in the village should go out and gather wood and bring it to his wigwam. The girl who gathered the right kind would become his son's wife. So the young girls went out after wood and they brought back many kinds—birch, cedar, spruce, basswood, pine, balsam.

In this village, there was a homely young girl who lived with her grandmother. The Homely One asked her grandmother, "Don't you think that I should try to gather wood too?"

"No," answered the grandmother. "The ogema wouldn't choose you . . . . . But if you want to, I'll help you, my child."

The next day the grandmother helped the Homely One make a tumpline to carry wood on her back. Then the girl went out and brought in almost every kind of wood, but the grandmother said, "Go out and find the tag alder that grows on the edge of the creek."

The Homely One wondered why she should gather that scrub tree, the tag alder. But she did as her grandmother told her. She found the tag alder and made a bundle of the wood, as much as she could carry on her back, and started out for the wigwam of the chief.

When the Homely One passed along on her way, the young girls laughed at her. They called out, "Look at the Homely One! Does she think that the ogema will choose her bundle of wood?"

But the Homely One kept on, and she placed her bundle before the chief. Her tag alder was just the kind of wood he wanted. The ogema knew that to gather a bundle of tag alder was not easy.

From that moment, the Homely One was changed into a beautiful young girl, the prettiest that anyone had ever seen, and she married the ogema's son.

13

THE LITTLE BOY and the WINDIGO

The story about the little boy and the windigo includes two incidents well known in folk literature. There is the incident of an eating contest in which the boy deceives a stupid and wicked giant by means of a bag provided for the food. Then there is the situation where the boy encourages the giant, through deception, to kill himself. The narrator commented at the outset that she was going to tell an Indian "Jack and the Beanstalk" story, and in a broad sense this is true, since a boy outwits a giant through cleverness and deception.

The story teller also explained that a windigo is a giant that eats people. We heard windigo lore on all of the northern Minnesota reservations. We heard that a man or woman might be changed into a windigo during times of severe cold and hunger. Such a transformation could also result from dreaming about a windigo. An antidote for these transformations was to have the individual affected consume hot tallow.

On one of the reservations we heard windigo lore that is associated with a particular place. Older Indians once said that at the bottom of a lake located on Cass Lake's Star Island there was a windigo medicine man. Many drownings were thus accounted for, and the lake became known and feared as Lake Windigo. The windigo is therefore a very real part of the Ojibwa setting in the story that follows.

*   *   *   *

Once upon a time there was an Indian village. The men were all hunters. One time some men went hunting and never returned. Then others went and the same thing happened. It kept on like that until the people said, "What are we going to do? Why do the hunters never return?" "There's a giant in the woods," some of them said.

There was a little boy who lived with his grandmother.

"Grandmother, can I go hunting? Give me a little sack of buckskin to carry my lunch."

"Don't you know there's a giant in the woods?"

He coaxed and coaxed his grandmother, and finally she gave him some dry venison in his pouch for his lunch. He was brave as a man.

"The giant will catch you," said the grandmother.

"Oh, no," answered the little boy, "I'm going to get him myself."

The little boy hunted for several days and there was no giant yet. But one day they met. The giant thought, "He's too small to eat. I will invite him to come to my place."

Windigo, the giant, ordered everything he could to eat. "Eat as much as I do, and I won't eat you, and you will be as big as I am."

The little boy thought, "What shall I do?"

They started eating, and they ate and they ate. Then the little boy thought of his pouch and he switched it in front of him around his neck. He made believe he was eating, but all the time he was dropping the food into his pouch. And the buckskin pouch kept on stretching. (Buckskin does that when it gets wet.)

Windigo thought, "My! My! The little boy eats as much as I do."

Finally Windigo gave up. He couldn't eat any more. Then the giant's old lady put on more food to eat. "Can you eat any more?" Windigo asked.

15

The little boy kept on eating and puffed out more and more. Then he said, "You can't slit your belly like I can," and he slit open his pouch. Windigo took out his hunting knife and tried to do the same thing.

So it was that in this way the little boy killed the giant, the Windigo.

THE RESCUE of the LOVELY PRINCESS

An elderly Ojibwa Episcopalian minister told us the story of "The Rescue of the Lovely Princess." He recalled that as a young boy of seven or eight, he heard the tale from an old man who was often invited over to the family wigwam to be the story teller for the evening. Later on when our narrator read the story of Aladdin in books at school, he was amazed to find there the genii and the magic lamp.

Seldom does one come upon a narrative told with greater ease and economy than here in "The Rescue of the Lovely Princess."

* * * *

Once upon a time a princess was carried away from her home. The prince wanted to find her and so he rubbed the magic lamp, and a genii appeared.

The genii said, "It will be a long and difficult quest." He directed the prince to the sea shore, and a monstrous bird, a big hawk, or an eagle, came.

The prince climbed on the eagle's back, and the eagle flew over the ocean day after day. It got very tired and weak. The prince saw a boy down below. The eagle swooped down, and the prince asked the boy for his fish.

The prince gave four or five fish to the eagle, and so

16

again the eagle had strength to fly. Finally it landed on a lonely island. There the prince found his princess a prisoner in the castle. An evil man held her there.

The prince killed the evil man and released the lovely princess.

THE OGEMA'S SON

The story of "The Ogema's Son" demands that the listener (or reader) suspend all disbelief, for here is the unreal world of a king, his wonderful son, and a magician; of *three* as the enchanted number and a mysterious and remote locale; of a hero tested with strange questions that he must not answer, a helpful snake, and then finally the transformation when the magic spell is broken.

* * * *

Once upon a time there lived a great king who had one son. This king or ogema loved his son very much. He loved him dearly and he wanted to do something for his son because he was so precious. One day the ogema called his men together. He asked the magician, "What can you do for this wonderful boy?"

The magician said, "Put him out of sight. Put him in hiding for three days. Don't go to see him. If you go, you'll lose him." So the king said he would put him away.

He put the prince in a castle that had just one window. The prince looked out of the window and far off he saw men on horseback. The men went in one direction only, day after day, and they never came back.

The king was lonesome for his son, but he did not go to see him. On the third day the prince came out of hiding, and there before the castle door was a horse with a beautiful saddle of gold and silver. He rode home on his horse and when he reached there, they had a big feast for him. Afterwards the prince was given the horse, all sparkling with the gold and silver saddle.

The boy then said goodbye to his father. "I am going away," he said. The boy and the horse went straight on the road that he had seen from the castle. On and on they went. The boy tried to find the marks of the horses that he had seen going up the road. The marks went only one way.

The prince traveled on for many days. Finally at sunset he came to the end of the road. Some horses were around. Some bones of horses too, and some horses dying from thirst and hunger. The prince wondered. He kept looking around. He saw a building and went in. No one was there. When he looked around inside, he heard a voice say, "So you're here!"

The prince looked around again and saw no one.

Then the voice said, "Come here."

The prince went farther, and in the corner he saw a snake curled up. The snake said to him, "You listen to what I'm going to tell you. Do just what I tell you, and then we will both live. Tonight as you sit here, all at once you will hear a roaring fire and there will be a man standing there. But don't talk to that man. He will ask you all kinds of questions. If you answer him, you will die."

It happened just as the snake had said. There was a fire, there was a man, and the man asked questions. But the prince never answered the man. Toward morning he was so tired that he nearly did answer him.

18

Finally it got to be morning and the man hit the prince, and the prince went under. Later a voice said, "Get up! Take care of your horse. Water it. Near a lake you will find good pasture."

The prince still kept wondering about the snake. The second night the same thing happened. The roaring fire, the thing that looked like a man, the questions—everything happened as the night before.

Again the prince was hit by the guy. Again the voice, "Get up! Take care of your horse." The snake this time was half a person. The snake said, "Just one more night and we'll conquer this."

The prince became anxious that night would come and that the third and last night of trial would be over. The same terrible roar of fire came, and he saw what looked like a big lion. The prince sat down and folded his hands and said, "I'll conquer this."

All night the prince was questioned. One answer would ruin him. When morning came, he saw that it really was a lion. "So you're not going to talk to me," said the lion and he hit the prince so hard that he thought he had killed him.

The prince was awakened by someone shaking him. He was still dazed, but he heard a voice say, "Go take your horse and go home."

When he finally came to, he saw a most beautiful woman. The prince had conquered the lion who once had turned the lovely princess into a snake.

The prince took the princess to his father's home. They rode back on the beautiful horse. When they came to the ogema's palace, there was a great feast and a great wedding.

O, MARIE

"O, Marie" was told to us by an eighty-two year old woman of Ojibwa and French Canadian background. She had lived during her childhood on Lake Superior's Madeline Island, long a stronghold of the Ojibwa. It was her Indian grandmother and in turn, her mother who maintained the custom of story telling in the family. Some of the tales told in their wigwam were about Nanabozho, the Ojibwa culture hero, and some were narratives like "O, Marie" and "Linda." The latter kind our story teller seemed to remember particularly well. She had learned her material in the Ojibwa language, and therefore she had to translate as she related the events.

"O, Marie" appears here the way the narrator told it to us on our unannounced visit. It includes details that are traditional in folk literature—the sword above the head, the beautiful young girl kept isolated, children born with a star on the forehead, and the helpful animal. The pathos and tenderness and the dramatic quality in the narrative style are memorable.

*   *   *   *

A man had a wife and a child. The wife always stayed at home. She worked hard and did all the chores.

In another room was O, Marie—a sister of the husband. No one ever saw her, and so no one knew how pretty she was.

One evening an old lady witch came to see the wife. The witch asked, "Don't you get tired working all the time?

Your sister-in-law lives only in silks, and while you work, she sleeps."

Then the witch said, "Kill all of one thing in one day. Kill all of the chickens. When your husband comes home, he will be angry. Tell him it was O,Marie who did this. Then he will chase her out."

When the husband came home in the evening, his wife was crying. "Look at what O,Marie did to us," she said. "O, Marie killed all our chickens."

The next day the wife killed all of the pigs. When the husband came home, she was crying her head off. "Look at what O, Marie did to us," she said. "O, Marie killed all our pigs."

The next day the wife killed all of the cows. Again she was crying when the 'husband came home, and she said, "Look at what O, Marie did to us. She killed all our cows."

The next day it was the same thing with the horses. Still the husband didn't get angry.

After awhile the witch came again. This time she told the Mrs. (that is, O, Marie's brother's wife) to kill her own child. The witch said, "Wash the baby and dress her up in white. Put her on a platter and then cut her throat."

The Mrs. did what the witch told her to do, but afterwards she cried.

The witch said, "See the door where O, Marie lives. Put drops of blood on the floor up to the door. Then go inside and hang this bloody sword over O, Marie's head."

The Mrs. did as the witch said. When the husband came home and saw all that had been done, he went to

O, Marie's room and opened the door. He saw how pretty O, Marie was—pretty as an angel. "O, Marie, sister!" he called out. "You have been doing all of these things all this time."

Then he told her to put her arms on a block, and he chopped off her hands. He threw her hands far out the door, and said, 'You must look for your hands. Now go!"

But before she left, O, Marie spoke to her brother. "A white pine will grow under your foot. When I find my hands, the tree will fall off."

O, Marie started out. She wandered and wandered. She had to live from tree roots and whatever she could find. After while she didn't know where she was. Then she heard some one coming toward her. It was a white nursing goat, and she got milk from it.

O, Marie stood there under a tree until she had strength enough to go on. 'Go straight," the goat said, "until you come to where there is a city. At the end of the town, there is a prince living. You crawl into the house of the prince's dog, and this dog will take care of you."

O, Marie went straight to the city, and everything happened as the goat had said. The prince's dog helped her. He saw that the table in the palace was all set, and the coffee all poured out. He went into the palace and grabbed a cup full of hot coffee, carried it out to O, Marie, and then brought the cup back to the palace.

The maid told the prince what the dog had done. The dog did the same thing again. So the prince told the maid to see what was in the dog's house, and there she found a beautiful girl, O, Marie. The maid told the prince and then

22

came back to the dog's house. She washed and bandaged O, Marie's sore arms, and she brought clean clothes.

In the meantime, the prince was getting ready to go to war. He told the maid, "Take good care of the girl. I want to marry her when I come back."

After while the prince came back from the war. He married O, Marie and then soon he had to go to war again.

"Wait on O, Marie like a child," he told the maid.

O, Marie had twins—two beautiful boys. Each one was born with a star on his forehead.

A colored man was working at the palace[1]. The maid said to him, "Bring this message to the prince: 'O, Marie is all right. You have beautiful twin boys. Each was born with a star on his forehead.' Keep going until you find the prince. Don't stop anywhere."

The colored man started. He kept going. He didn't go anywhere to sleep. But one day when he was sleeping outside at sundown, an old lady came along. She searched him, and she found the note about O, Marie and the beautiful twin boys. The old lady (the same witch as before) changed the message, so that it read: "One boy is a dog. The other is human." Then she sent this note with the colored man instead of the right one.

The colored man reached the prince and gave him the

---

[1] The unusual situation of "a colored man" as a character in an Ojibwa story might possibly be related to the following facts: A Negro named Jean Bonga came to Mackinac in 1782 as a servant of Captain Robertson, a British officer. When Robertson died, Jean Bonga was freed. His son Pierre married into the Ojibwa tribe, and Pierre's son George became a wealthy trader at Fond du Lac.

note without looking at it. The prince sent back the message: "Keep them until I get home."

The same thing happened as before. The old lady witch took the note from the colored man when he was sleeping. She changed the message to: "Send them away. I don't want ever to see them."

This was the message that came back to the palace. O, Marie cried when she read it. She didn't tell anyone what the note said, but she told the maid that she wanted to go away before the prince returned.

O, Marie tied the twins to herself and started out. They watched her from the palace until they could see her no longer.

O, Marie walked and walked all night. She was thirsty, and the babies were crying. She walked until she came to a beautiful creek. The water was clear. O, Marie tried to reach the water, but she couldn't. She leaned far over. The babies fell off her, and she hit the water. When she came up, she had her hands.

Now I shall take you back. O, Marie's brother was dying. A white pine grew under his foot after O, Marie left his house and now the tree dropped off his foot. (It was just at the moment that O, Marie got her hands again.) The brother said, "O, Marie never did anything wrong." And then his wife told him how the witch had told her to do all those terrible things and blame O, Marie for them.

After O, Marie got her hands, she cut saplings with the knife that she had been given at the palace, and she made a grass wigwam, a wigwam of reeds. She made a bow and arrows (this is a story, you know) and killed game for food.

Meanwhile the prince came back to the palace, and he found out that O, Marie had left.

"Which way did she go?" he asked.

"Over in that direction," the maid answered.

"I am not coming back," the prince said. "Where I find the bones of my boys, I stay."

One day when O, Marie was weaving mats, she saw the prince coming on a horse. "Oh, no," she thought. "It can't be. It must be someone else."

Then the prince asked, "O, Marie, is that you?"

And so the prince found O, Marie and his beautiful twin boys.

LINDA

Upon finishing "O, Marie," the narrator described the story "Linda" and asked us to come back another time to hear it. She said that it was a long story, that it used to take a whole evening "to tell it in Chippewa," and that she had not thought of it for years. We came back within two weeks' time, and seated around our narrator's kitchen stove on a cold evening in November, we heard the account of Linda.

The story teller spoke deliberately, partly because she was translating and partly also, it seemed, because she had a regard for precision even within the framework of the purely fanciful. In the sequence of events, there is a logical incorporation of such incidents and motifs from folk literature as the beast with many heads, the three princesses delivered from the underworld, help given by means of an unusual object (the golden bugle), and testimony or verification by means of a slipper, a ring, or a handkerchief.

* * * *

Once upon a time (that is the way it would start), once upon a time there was a big city where kings lived. Then it happened that some great animal destroyed the city (that is, the people in it), all except one king and the king's wife and their daughter Linda.

The king thought the world of his daughter. He built a castle many stories high, and in the highest room he kept his daughter. No one could see her. They couldn't even hear her voice.

And so once upon a time, a young prince came from far off to see Linda, and the king wouldn't let him. The prince tried to call from outside the castle, and Linda couldn't hear his voice. So he went away.

Then another prince came. He had heard about Linda, and he asked the king if he could talk to the beautiful girl, but the king wouldn't let him. So this prince did the same as the other. He went away too.

Another prince came. There were three altogether who came. Each time the same thing happened, and all went back.

Then the king had his servants move Linda down to the cellar—to a place where no one could get in from any direction. Linda stayed there a long time. She had servants and just lived.

One evening, quite a while after, she heard a window-rap. She got up and went to the window, and she saw a nice young prince standing outside. He said, "Hello, my girl, how are you?"

Linda answered, "I'm all right, but I don't know who you are."

The prince replied, "That's all I want to know."

Three times the prince came, and the last time he had a little bundle in his hand. "Give this to my son," the prince said.

Then came the time for the child to be born, and it was a boy. After while, Linda found the bundle that the prince had left for his son. Linda opened it and found a golden bow and arrow.

Later the boy played outside with the bow and arrow, and the king was proud that his grandson could shoot so well.

One day the grandfather brought the boy to the yard to see all the chickens, and then the boy killed all the chickens with his golden bow and arrow. The servants told the king, but he just said, "Oh, it's all right. We'll get some more."

The king brought his grandchild to the yard to see all the horses. Then the grandchild killed all the horses with his golden bow and arrow.

The king brought the boy to the yard to see all the cows, and the boy killed all the cows with his golden bow and arrow.

One day the king took his grandson to a big clearing which was the place where once upon a time the big city stood. The king said, "Never come this far to play. It is dangerous. Once upon a time a big animal came here and destroyed the city."

After while the boy wondered, "Why not go that far

to play?" So he kept on going out toward the big clearing, and he wandered around until he got tired.

The boy sat down on a big mossy log to rest. Then he noticed that the log was moving. He got up and looked around and then tried to sit again. He got up and this time—the third time—he saw a shape like a head at the end of the log.

The head spoke to the boy, "Will you do me a favor? Will you shoot me on my neck with your golden bow and arrow?" Three times the head asked this, and each time the boy started to shoot but then couldn't make himself do it.

Finally the head said, "I'll give you all my strength. There'll be no one stronger than you in the world."

So at the fourth time the boy shot the head. He cut it right off. The head started out, and the boy followed it down to where it hit the trees and made a mark. The boy then followed these marks. He broke his bow and arrow and threw them away.

The boy followed the head until he got to a big wide road and there he stood a while thinking which way to go. While standing, he heard someone singing and laughing. Then he heard a wagon coming and men talking. Soon he saw an oxen team and three men driving the team. When they got nearer, one of them said to the boy, "Hello, where do you come from?"

The boy answered, "Just around here." And then he asked the men where they were going.

The three Frenchmen said that they were going out hunting, and they told the boy that he could go along if he wanted to. So the boy got into the wagon with them.

They rode a ways, and then they saw a house standing along side the road. The men thought that this would be a good place to stop while they hunted.

The next morning they arranged for one of them to stay at home while the rest went to hunt in the woods. The oldest of the men said, "I'll stay home today." The other two and the boy went out.

In a little while, the man that stayed at home heard some one coming. He wondered. He thought that the Frenchmen must have forgotten something and were coming back. While he was wondering, a short man with a beard clear down to his foot came in.

The bearded man said, "This is my house. Get out." The two got into a fight, and the old man—the one who stayed home to cook—was knocked out for most of the day. The bearded man left. That night the cook did not tell the others what had happened.

The next day another one of the Frenchmen stayed home to cook, and the others left to hunt. The same thing happened. The bearded man came. He said, "This is my house. Get out." The two got into a fight, and the cook was knocked out for most of the day. The men came back. After supper they sat around and talked about their hunting, but the cook didn't say what had happened to him.

The third day the third Frenchman stayed home, and the same thing happened.

The boy was the last one to stay home to cook. He washed the breakfast dishes, he made the beds, he swept the floor, and then as he worked, he heard someone outside.

29

It was the bearded man. He came in. He said, "Get out. This is my house."

The boy and the bearded man fought. But the boy had strength. He had the power given to him by the head, and he knocked the bearded man out and then threw him on a big limb.

When the three Frenchmen came back, the boy told what had happened, and after that, each one told about the day when he had stayed home to cook.

But the three hunters wouldn't believe the boy. "Show us," they said.

The boy took them where he had left the bearded man, but the bearded man was gone. Then they set out to follow the drops of blood to find him.

This is the way it is told. They came to a rock—the last place where they saw the drops of blood. The three Frenchmen tried to pull the rock to see where the bearded man went, but they couldn't budge it.

One said, "We'll get the oxen." But the oxen couldn't move the rock either. They wondered.

The boy said, "Let me try."

The Frenchmen laughed. "Even the oxen couldn't. How could you?" But the boy got hold of the rock and threw it aside. This was the gift of strength that he had from the head.

Where the rock had been, they looked down into a big hole. They could see the blood that showed where the bearded man had gone.

So the Frenchmen wanted to know, "What's down in that hole?"

They had the oldest one go down with a rope tied

30

around his waist. "If you see anything, shake the rope. We'll pull you up."

The old Frenchman went down a ways. He got afraid and started to shake the rope. "He must see something," they said. "Pull him up."

But when he came up, he said that he had seen nothing. It was just dark down there.

Then the second oldest went down. He went a little farther, shook the rope, and they pulled him up. He hadn't seen anything either. The same thing happened with the third Frenchman.

So they asked the boy if he wanted to go down. "Yes, I'll try," he said.

He went down, clear down. He saw nothing. It was all dark. He got his feet on the ground. He felt around. He felt a doorknob and went into a room. It was bright as the sun in the room where he went in.

He saw a beautiful woman, the prettiest he had ever seen. She spoke. "Why do you come here? You'll be killed by the animal."

Then she offered him the sword above her head. He took it. Waited. He heard a noise like the wind coming. It was a big animal. She told him to cut the head with a sword. He cut one. Another formed. He cut the second one.

Then the boy told her, "Get ready. I am coming back after you."

He saw another door. In this room was another beautiful girl, younger than the first. The same thing happened as before. The girl said that there would be four heads formed. The animal came like a tornado. That was the way it sounded to the boy. The boy cut off one head.

Another formed. After the fourth head, he told the girl, "Get ready. I am coming back after you."

Then he opened another door, and it happened the same as before. The girl in this room was younger still, and she was beautiful. She said that there would be eight heads formed. The animal came like a tornado, and the boy cut off a head. Another one formed. He cut off eight heads in all, and by that time he was tired.

He tied the oldest girl to the rope, then the next, and the next, and then himself. He shook the rope, and the three Frenchmen up above said, "There must be something down there."

The Frenchmen had to use their oxen to pull up the heavy load on the rope. They took the first girl off, the second, and the third. Then they cut the rope, and the boy went all the way down again.

He got knocked out when he fell on the ground. He came to, and then he saw the first door again. He found a slipper, picked it up, and put it in his pocket. He went in the next room, and he found a ring with a name on it. He put the ring in his pocket.

He went into the third room. Here he found a handkerchief and a golden bugle. He wondered what the bugle was for. He tried it. Heard nothing. He tried it a second time. Same thing—he heard nothing. The third time he heard a noise like a tornado, and there was the bearded man.

"What do you want me for?" he asked.

The boy said, "I want to go up above."

Then the bearded man told the boy a story. It was about the three Frenchmen. They were going to marry the three girls. This was to be in a city nearby. The bearded man told the boy to go first to a blacksmith at the end of the town. The blacksmith would hire him.

"If you have any trouble," the bearded man said, "blow three times. I'll be there with you."

So the boy started toward the city. He went to the blacksmith, and the blacksmith hired him. The next day the blacksmith told the boy about the three daughters of the king who had been kidnapped when they were young and now they were to be married to three Frenchmen. These men said that they had rescued the girls.

The blacksmith worked for the king, and now he was asked to make a shoe for the oldest daughter. The shoe was to be a slipper to take the place of one that the girl left behind. The slipper had to match exactly. All the materials would be furnished.

The blacksmith didn't know what to do. How could he make a slipper? So he asked the boy, and the boy said that he would try if he could be alone all day as he worked.

The next day the boy had the slipper that was made to match the other. The blacksmith was pleased. He said, "I'll bring it to the king's daughter." And the king's daughter saw that the slipper was a perfect match.

Then the blacksmith was hired to make a ring for the second daughter. The girl's name had to be on the ring. Again he asked the boy, and again the boy said, "I'll try, if I can be alone all day at my work."

The next day the blacksmith brought the ring to the king's daughter, and she noticed that it was her own. "This is the ring that I left behind."

The king asked the blacksmith to make a handkerchief

33

for the third daughter. It was to be of a certain kind of cloth, and her name was to be embroidered on it.

As before, the blacksmith asked the boy if he would make the handkerchief, and the boy said, "I'll try, if I can be alone all day at my work."

The next day the blacksmith brought the handkerchief to the king's daughter, and she saw that it was her own— the handkerchief that she had forgotten.

The three Frenchmen were to be married to the king's daughters on the next day. But now the daughters asked their father, "Why shouldn't we have a party first and invite everybody—the blacksmith, the blacksmith's boy, everybody?"

Their father—the king—said, "Yes, whatever you wish."

So they had the party. The boy didn't want to go, but the blacksmith made him. On opposite sides of the table were the three Frenchmen and the three women. The king was at the head.

While the party was going on, the daughters asked their father if each one could say something about his life, tell his story. The king said 'yes" and so the people started. The Frenchmen told about their lives and about how they had rescued the king's daughters.

It came to the blacksmith's turn and then the boy's. The boy asked if the servants would put an extra plate beside him. "I have a friend I can call," he said.

The women knew then that this was the boy who had helped them.

The boy blew the golden bugle three times, and the bearded man stood beside him. The bearded man told about how he had taken the girls and how the boy had saved them.

The king then asked his daughters what they wanted to do. The youngest said that she wanted to marry the boy. The second one wanted to marry the blacksmith. And the older daughter found someone too, and they all lived happy lives.

LEGENDARY HISTORY

We were told two versions of how the Indians came to North America. Both of them give a feeling of the passage of a long period of time. The first version names the bear, one of the largest dodems (totems), as the ancestor of the early people. Dodems were kinship groups or clans, each of which was perpetuated by a symbol of the particular animal, bird, fish, reptile. The child inherited the kinship group from his father. According to the tradition, marriages were not to take place between members of the same dodem. The bear, marten, lynx, eagle, loon, crane, bullhead, and sturgeon were dodems represented by our story tellers.

* * * *

HOW the INDIANS got into NORTH AMERICA
(First Version)

Two girls were out swimming. They would swim and dive and sun themselves. Then they got into a canoe. They were very tired. The canoe was being blown out into the ocean. The land disappeared. The girls drifted and traveled for days and days. A bird came along and fed them. Another bird brought them water.

Finally they landed. They got off and went in search of

human life. Again they traveled for years and years. They grew tired and older. One said, "We're growing old. You go that way and I'll go this way."

They parted. One traveled alone for years and never married. The other met a bear and married him. They had children and they spread over North America. Today the bear dodem numbers many Ojibwa Indians.

* * * *

(Second Version)

A long time ago the Indians were hungry for deer, so they set out on a hunt. The women and the children went along with them. For many days they searched for game, but they had no success.

They went farther and farther away from their camping ground until they reached the ocean shore. Then they saw deer far off in the distance. They got into their canoes and paddled toward the image.

Suddenly a wind arose and drove the canoes farther away from where they had started. The Indians battled with the winds for four years and finally the storm drove them to the shore of North America.

STORIES TOLD TO TEACH

The Ojibwa were a people who believed in the use of story for the express purpose of teaching traditions and conduct. Sometimes the aim was to teach the children, and sometimes the parents. The stories of the robin, the oriole, and the owl which are presented here illustrate both types. It is of interest that each is about a bird.

HE Who OVER-DREAMED

To appreciate the story of "He Who Over-Dreamed," one needs to keep in mind the significant custom of fasting as it was carried out among the early Indians. An old man living on the Mille Lacs Reservation explained how one morning when he was seven years old, he found some ashes on his dish. His father expected him to rub the ashes on his face and then leave for an isolated place to have a dream. If he should dream of an animal, that animal then became his manido or dream spirit (or guardian spirit). The fast at the time of puberty was particularly important in a boy's life.

The teller of the story "He Who Over-Dreamed" explained that the young boy had already gone out into the woods many times to fast and he had dreamed about everything there was to dream about. When the father insisted that his son blacken his face and fast still more, the young boy obeyed, but he had fasted too long and he became a robin.

The narrative contains instruction for both parents and children. Here again, one needs to understand the people from whom the story comes, for the lesson reflects the Ojibwa belief that one should not ask Kijie manido for too much. One should instead be grateful for that which is provided.

*   *   *   *

A young man went into the woods to fast so that he could have a dream. He had his dream and then he returned to the wigwam. His father asked him to go back and fast longer, and so the boy went on with his fasting.

When he again returned to the wigwam, the father urged him to fast for one more day.

But even after the one day, the boy could not eat. He had fasted so long. The boy fixed himself some paint and painted his face and combed his hair, so he would look like the robin (o-pe-che). "I'm going to be a robin," he said.

He had his wish. He was turned into a robin and flew up on the cross-beams in the wigwam.

"Son, son, come back. Come back!" the father cried.

But the boy answered, "No, I'm going to be a robin. I will come back in the spring and then I will feel it in my breast if the summer will be good or bad, or if there will be war."

* * * *

THE BOY WHO TURNED into an ORIOLE

The story about the boy who became an oriole was evidently told to warn mothers to stay home and care for their children. We heard the story at Fond du Lac, a region which according to early settlers had many beautiful birds, including the colorful oriole.

* * * *

A woman often went away and left her baby at home. The little boy used to cry, "Stay home! Stay home!" He cried and he cried, but the mother would not stay home.

One day the little boy said, "I wish I could be something else."

"Son, son," the mother answered, but still she went away.

"Stay home! Stay home!" the boy kept saying.

One day when the mother returned she saw not her son. But instead she saw a half bird and half boy flying

up to the cross-beams of the wigwam. He had changed
into an oriole—part black and part orange.

The mother heard him sing:

Ah-bin ah-bin ah-bin
Ningwis ninga nindig
Stay home stay home stay home
My son my mother tells me

* * * *

THE OWL and the LITTLE GIRL

The narrative 'The Owl and the Little Girl" appears
here in two versions. Most, although not all, of our informants had heard the story from their mothers or
grandmothers. Some of the Ojibwa remembered being
told that if they were not good, the owl (ko-ko-o-o) would
carry them away. The owl was also used as a threat to
keep children close to the wigwam. One old man recalled
his mother saying, "If you go to the sugar bush at night,
the owl will come and carry you away in his ear." Besides
the owl, Ojibwa parents used the Sioux and also the
Frenchman (or any other white man) as a warning or
threat. We were told how important it was for children to
be taught to be quiet, for sometimes it could be a matter of
life or death.

The "owl story" is here in two versions. The second of
the two suggests that the threat might turn on the parents.

* * * *

(First Version)

The mother told her little girl that the owl would come
and get her if she didn't behave, but the little girl did not
believe this. So one day the mother lifted the blanket that

39

covered the opening of the wigwam, and said, "Come on, owl, and get this little girl."

The little girl said, "I'm not afraid of the owl."

One day when the mother heard the owl hooting around the wigwam, she thought that she would frighten her little girl, so she put her outside. Later on when the mother went to bring her in again, she could not find her.

The little girl was gone for four years. The mother looked everywhere for her and finally she asked the medicine man. He went into a trance and dreamed about the girl. He said, "She's all right, though she's at a house and I cannot get in."

Then one summer the little girl came home. The mother wanted to know where she had been. She was dressed well and she seemed to be well fed. The little girl said that she had been in a tree and that she was given all kinds of meat to eat, rabbit and other kinds. So the mother thought the owl must have taken her and cared for her.

(Second Version)

A little girl would not obey her mother. "Come on, owl, and take this little girl."

The owl said, "No, I can't take your child."

This happened many times. Then the owl finally said, "All right," and he took the little girl to his nest.

The little girl was gone for a long time, and the mother started looking everywhere for her.

After many years the owl said, "Your mother is lonesome for you. I'll take you back to her."

The owl took the girl back. The mother noticed that her daughter had been well cared for while she was gone.

Never again did the mother tell her children that the owl would get them.

STORIES ABOUT OLD TURTLE

The two Old Turtle stories that appear here are decidedly different. The first contains the tortoise-hare motif, while the other is in some respects similar to "The Homely One" in the "Once upon a Time" section.

OLD TURTLE and the RABBIT

We found the story of the race between the turtle and the rabbit or hare to be a controversial one. A few of the Ojibwa said that while Indians like to tell the story, it "isn't really Indian." Two of the narrators, whose parents and grandparents were of the Mide tradition, opposed the story on different grounds. They maintained that an Ojibwa would not tell tales about either Turtle or Rabbit, because both animals were considered too sacred to be talked about at all, or talked about light-heartedly. Several informants said that Turtle was one of the chiefs of the animal world and that he was prominent in magic practices. The shaking-tent ceremony would be an illustration. (This ceremony is explained in the last section of the book.)

* * * *

One winter day Rabbit asked Old Turtle to run a race with him. They started out on the ice. Rabbit ran ahead very fast, and Old Turtle plopped into a hole in the ice and swam along in the water. Every once in a while he came up out of a hole and looked around for Rabbit. One time he saw that Rabbit was resting. This time Old Turtle

41

plopped into the water again and swam ahead and won the race.

THE HOMELY ONE (OLD TURTLE)

Here again is a story called "The Homely One," but this time Old Turtle is the main character. The narrative reflects his resourcefulness in gathering wood and in catching the red iron (or copper, as our story teller explained). It also reflects Old Turtle's unpopularity. He is the unwanted one, no matter how well he carries out the courtship tests. That Old Turtle should even aspire to marry the chief's daughter was a source of amusement to our eighty-nine year old narrator. Turtle was evidently once held in esteem or awe as a powerful manido in the Mide religion or as a chief in the animal world, but he is also a character in a number of Ojibwa adventure tales. The humor in these stories is frequently crude, and the adventure often fiercely competitive. Old Turtle is likely to be assertive, resourceful, and clever, but at the same time the target for laughter. Although he is generally unpopular with the other characters, his ingenuity is not to be discounted. The story that follows needs to be interpreted in the light of Old Turtle as a character in Ojibwa folk tales.

In fact, Ojibwa customs and environment are reflected in several ways, just as they were in the other story with the same title. (See the "Once upon a Time" section.) The custom of the courtship tests has already been explained. Once again, gathering the right kind of wood is a test around which action revolves. In the story that follows, it is important to know that wa-dup, or spruce root, was

42

greatly valued by the Indians, since it was used as a strong thread in making canoes. Old Turtle, however, had to pass a second test, the catching of red iron, or copper. Ojibwa life is reflected here too. One of our story tellers proudly described how the early Ojibwa used to be able to temper copper. At Fond du Lac, the home of the narrator, copper nuggets have been found along the St. Louis River.

The two courtship tests taken by Old Turtle form almost independent episodes. Thus the structure of the Old Turtle narrative differs from that of the other "Homely One."

* * * *

The chief wanted to marry his daughter, so he decided to give her to the one who brought him the right kind of wood. Everyone went out to see what they could find. Old Turtle went out too, and he came in carrying a bundle of wa-dup on his back.

The chief said, "I don't think that you should marry my daughter." So Old Turtle lost out. He was so homely.

Then the chief said, "Whoever can catch red iron in a net shall marry my daughter."

So Old Turtle went out again along with all the others. As he left, the chief said to him, "Go that way."

But Old Turtle said to himself, "Right here, right here, I can set a net."

Others let red iron go by, but Old Turtle caught red iron in his net.

He brought red iron back to the chief, but the chief said, "I don't think you should marry my daughter."

So Old Turtle lost again. He was so homely. He got his red iron all for nothing.

43

A STORY OF ANIMAL WARFARE
The Crabs Go to War

In the story "The Crabs Go to War," the animals become aggressive and organize a war party. Thus we have here the well-known motif of animal warfare.

We think it significant that we received a comparatively full version of this tale. The teller stopped her dishwashing, sat down at the kitchen table, and transported us all into the world of the crabs or the crawfish. The narrative stands on its own merit as recorded, but it was greatly enhanced for us by the story teller's animation and her rhythmic gestures.

* * * *

Some crabs were going to make war on the raccoon. The young warriors wanted adventure. The old men said, "Why don't you young people paint your faces, put feathers in your hair, and fast and learn something about war?"

One young crab went out to look for his prey. He found what he thought was a dead raccoon. It was covered with dry tree rot. The young crab went back and told the others to come to see what he had found in the woods.

The young warriors were ready to march to the place where the raccoon was, but a lady crab who had had her hands bitten off by a raccoon said, "Don't go, don't go!"

Some of the crabs said, "Don't listen to her."

The crabs marched on. They found the raccoon and formed in a circle around him. They picked at him with their spears. They sang, "Pick—jump! Pick—jump!" They kept picking at the raccoon and jumping back—picking and jumping back.

44

Then the raccoon jumped up and ate some of the crabs. Another raccoon came along, and the first raccoon told him to have his fill. This he did.

The little crabs said, "Come and eat us too!"

The first raccoon said, "I'm tired of eating big crabs." So he picked up the little crabs and went down to the water. He washed them and ate them all up.

To this day the raccoon washes his food before he eats it.

A VERSION OF THE BLOOD-BOY STORY

A hunter and his wife lived alone. They wanted a boy very badly. They had none.

One day when the hunter had killed an animal he kept on saying, "I wish I had a boy. I wish I had a boy."

As he was preparing the meat, some blood fell on his hand. Again he said, "I wish I had a boy." He kept on repeating, "I wish I had a boy." The blood began to form a human being—first legs, then arms, and then a head. Finally it began to breathe. The hunter took the boy down to the lake and washed it.

The boy grew into a beautiful man and a wonderful hunter. He was brave and thoughtful. He was wise and kind. He had wit. He was tireless. He was of the very best.

When the boy grew older, he said, "Father, I am going far away to look for some people. They live somewhere. I am going to look for them. My boat is ready for me on the lake shore."

The boat was beautiful. It was imbedded with seashells and pearls. It had a beautiful paddle—the most beautiful ever seen.

The boy told his mother and father goodbye. He pointed his arrow westward and set out. He traveled for many days. Then one day the boat went over the falls and he drowned.

They found the pearl-decked canoe and inside it, a man and a woman. They tried to revive them. They worked hard, but they lost them.

TWO VERSIONS OF A WIDESPREAD STORY
The Rolling Head

We are including two versions of the story "The Rolling Head." Each contributes to the other, although both are comparatively full.

The opening episode in the story reflects the traditional Ojibwa attitude toward an adulterous wife. The flight of the children introduces one of the most widely known motifs in the folk literature of the world. The first version contributes particularly here by giving the flight in greater detail. The second version includes the motif of escape over water by means of a crane bridge. Each time as we listened to the part about the obstacle flight, we realized that we were hearing a narrative enjoyed over the centuries by people in different parts of the world. Folklorists and anthropologists report that the obstacle flight motif appears in tales told in North and South America, Asia, the islands of the North Pacific, Africa, and Europe. In all probability, this motif and the narrative "The Rolling Head" will not exist much longer in oral form among the Ojibwa. It seems indeed that for this story and others, it is time's edge.

Both story tellers told about the old man (the evil

magician) who captures the older brother and takes him across the lake. The narrator of the second version included the burning of the clothes, a son-in-law motif found in North American Indian tales. Each narrator stressed the pitiful fate of the younger brother who becomes half wolf and half child.

* * * *

(First Version)

Once upon a time there was a hunter. Every evening when he came back, he found his little boy crying and sighing. He asked his wife, "Why is he crying?"

The mother said, "Oh, he just cries."

One evening when the father came home, he found the boy alone. "Why are you crying, my son?"

The little boy then told his father that another man kept coming to the wigwam and the mother went with him. Always before she left, she painted her face and put bear grease on her hair to make it glossy. Then she braided her hair and tied it with buckskin at the tip.

So the father hid himself and saw all this. Later the father and mother argued, and the father killed his wife.

The father went back to the wigwam and said to his son, "Now I know why you have been crying every day. I am leaving you. When you see the sun setting in the west, that means that I am dead too. You must leave right away and take Little Brother with you. Your mother's head will follow you. Do not listen to her. When Head comes close, throw thorns back. The thorn bushes will grow and cover Head. Each time Head will try again to follow you. Each time it will say, 'Wait! Wait!'

"The next time throw flint back, and the bushes will

47

break into flames and stop Head. Again you will hear Head say, 'Wait! Wait!' This time turn yourself into a mountain, and Head will again be stopped."

The boys started out. Soon they heard Head rolling. When it came near, they heard it call, "Wait! Wait! I want to nurse Little Brother." The boy thought what to do and threw the thorns back over his shoulder, and thorn bushes grew.

Three or four days went by and Big Brother heard Head again. This time he threw the flint back and the flaming bushes stopped Head.

Some time later he heard Head call again, "Wait! Wait! Let me nurse Little Brother." Then he remembered what his father had told him. He turned himself into a mountain, so Head could not get across. (Some Indians believe that this was the way mountains were made.)

Finally Big Brother came to the edge of a lake. He stopped there and made a bow and arrow for Little Brother to play with. They saw something floating out on the lake. Big Brother shot at it and hit the mother's head.

There was an old man in a canoe. He shoved Big Brother into the canoe and crossed the lake, and Little Brother was left on the shore alone. Little Brother kept crying, and started to yell like a wolf. "I'm turning into a wolf—I'm turning into a wolf!" he cried.

All this time Big Brother begged the old man to let him go back to look for Little Brother. But the old man would never let him go and he was forced to marry the old man's daughter.

Still Big Brother always wanted to go back to find Little Brother. When he heard the wolves howling, he thought of a plan. He told the old man, "Let us make a wigwam." This they did.

Then Big Brother laid some meat in the wigwam and made a noise like a wolf. The wolves came. More and more wolves came, and all the time Big Brother kept looking for Little Brother. Finally the half-wolf and half-child came. Big Brother knew him and fed him well.

Little Brother grew back into a child again.

*   *   *   *

(Second Version)

There were two little boys and a mother and father in this family. The man hunted all day long.

The little boys saw different men come to the wigwam to see the mother. They told their father, and he killed the mother.

Then he said to his sons, "Run away as soon as the clouds are red. You will know then that I am dead. Your mother's head will chase you. It will roll through thistles and through fire. Here is a spear to throw at the head, but it will keep on rolling.

"You will find some cranes at a lake cracking bugs. The cranes will make a bridge by putting their beaks together. Use this bridge to cross the water. The rolling head will try to cross this bridge too, but the cranes will let it fall into the lake."

All this happened as the father said.

Then one day the two boys were playing on the lake shore. The little brother started to cry, and the big brother made a bow and arrow for him. Then they saw a boat and an old man lying in the boat. And the old man took the big brother into the boat. He would not take the

49

little boy along. The big brother wanted the old man to wait for the little brother, but the old man would not wait.

The old man took the big brother across the lake and gave him to his daughter for a husband. Time and time and time again the older brother tried to get his little brother, but the old man kept him from doing this because he always called to the boat to come back. All the while the little brother was turning into a wolf.

The old man was mean and tricky. He tried in every way to keep the older brother from helping his little brother. He became so mean that after a while he wanted to get rid of his son-in-law too. One time when they were on a hunting trip the old man stole his son-in-law's clothes during the night and burned them.

On the next hunting trip the son-in-law planned to outfox the old man, and he took the old man's clothes and exchanged them for his own.

In the early morning when it was still dark, the old man got up and burned the clothes that he thought belonged to his son-in-law. The old man called out, "Get up! Get up! There's something burning."

The son-in-law got up. Then the old man found out that he had burned his own clothes.

The son-in-law went on his way. The old man built a fire by a rock to keep warm. The rock melted. It was so cold that the old man turned into a tamarack as he stood there.

ACCOUNTS OF SPIRIT WANDERERS AND LITTLE PEOPLE

The narrative "Man of the Wild Woods" (the first in the group that follows) tells about a spirit wanderer—restless, mysterious, and exacting. He has much in common with the Pagak (or Bagak), and since it is difficult to obtain information about this character in Ojibwa folk literature, we shall summarize here what we heard from a few of the story tellers: The Pagak used to wander restlessly in the woods as a skeleton, sometimes a flying skeleton. He was a sign of bad luck to anyone who saw him. One woman spoke of how with the coming of spring, the Indians kept very quiet and listened for the Pagak in the woods. They would hear him shoot, for he was a hunter, or they would hear his bones make a noise as he walked. Generally he was spoken of as the skeleton of a human being, although one person described him as monster-like in appearance.

This section also contains two short accounts of the little people of the water, thickets, woods, and cliffs. Usually we heard that the home of these tiny people (or pygmies) was under the hills. One informant said that the little people were especially mischievous on stormy nights. They caused no end of trouble. They themselves could never be seen, but the next morning their footprints in the sand along the lake shore gave evidence that they had been there.

These traditions of the Ojibwa are similar to those of other Indians and other races. Human beings have readily believed in the presence of unnatural, restless, often bargaining and ominous wanderers or in the existence of little

51

people who on occasion pour out of a hillside or mischievously sabotage man's efforts.

MAN of the WILD WOODS

There is a man in buckskin who goes about the lakes and woods. People see him and then he is gone.

One day when a hunter was out in the woods with his little dog—a black and white pup—the dog disappeared. After that the man became one of the very best hunters. The dog's disappearance signifies that the hunter had given his dog in return for his luck.

Sometimes people hear a whistle, or they hear their names called. But the minute they turn around, the man of the wild woods is gone . . . . . Or a rack of tools might fall over, but no one is there. A few people say that they have seen him and that sometimes he has smiled, but only for a second, and then he is gone.

Some say he is a spirit who is trying to get himself back into human form.

* * * *

THE LITTLE PEOPLE

Many times when the Indians are traveling in their canoes they see the strange little people, but they can never get near them. Sometimes the little people are in a canoe and sometimes they play on the cliffs along Lake Superior.

One time some Ojibwa saw some of these little men in a canoe on the lake. When the Indians tried to get near them, the little men jumped out of their canoe and ran up the cliff hiding their faces in their arms.

THE LITTLE PEOPLE and the HUNTER

One time an Indian killed a partridge and when he went to get it, it was gone. The little people had taken it away. The hunter could hear them laughing in the distance.

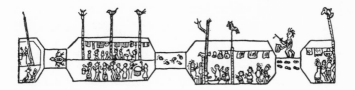

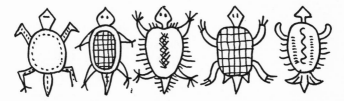

PART II

NANABOZHO, THE CENTRAL CHARACTER IN OJIBWA TALES

"The history of their eccentric grand incarnation—the great uncle of the red man—whom they term Man-abo-sho, would fill a volume of itself, which would give a more complete insight into their real character, their mode of thought and expression, than any book which can be written concerning them."

William Warren, HISTORY OF THE OJIBWAY NATION
(p. 27)

The old Ojibwa liked to tell us about Nanabozho, the one-time principal figure in Algonquian mythology, legendary history, and the Grand Medicine Society. But when we confronted them with the question "Who is Nanabozho?", they looked at us perplexed. They accept Nanabozho and his characteristics, inconsistent as these may be, and thus they found it difficult to reply. Most of them said that he is a powerful manido or spirit being. Some said he is the "Great Rabbit." One woman said, "He is both human and super-human." One of our youngest informants spoke of him as "a superman," and still another said, "Nanabozho is an ordinary Indian and an Indian extraordinary." Almost unanimously Nanabozho was mentioned as a brother to the animals, the plants, the trees, and the many different aspects of nature. As the legends show, Nanabozho has all of these characteristics and still others.

The Ojibwa beliefs about Nanabozho need to be viewed in relation to the traditional belief in a large number of manidos or spirit beings (good and evil) that were thought to exist everywhere in nature—in the animals, birds, trees, an odd-shaped rock, the waterfalls, thunder and lightning, the winds and the cardinal directions. The heavens and the earth and the layers above and below the earth were all the abode of the manidos. This entire concept rested on the belief that the natural and the supernatural were inseparable. Thus it can be seen how the natural world would be considered a source of spirit power.

The great majority of spirit beings were represented as animals. These animal spirits had the ability to change their form whenever they wished. To these supernatural beings the Ojibwa made offerings for appeasement. It is remembered that Nanabozho was called the Great Rabbit. He was also called the White Hare. The words *Great* and *White* refer to an early mythological time in which there were some animal manidos of unusual size and power. They were the largest of a species. Nanabozho was the greatest of all these great animals, but he had formidable enemies in the gigantic underwater manidos (such monsters as the Great Horned Snake or the Great Panther). On the side of Nanabozho in this long conflict were the good thunderbirds (also powerful manidos). "The thunderbirds helped Nanabozho chase the big snakes," was the explanation given by one of the Ojibwa we interviewed. Other Ojibwa told how they were brought up in fear of the evil underwater manidos. One woman (Wind Going Through the Clouds) said that she and her family never waded in the lake near their home unless they first put tobacco on the water as an offering to the good manidos for protection. The same woman stated emphatically, "There still *are* manidos."

Some of our informants spoke of Kijie manido (kind manido or in popular terminology, the Great Spirit) as the supreme being in the mythological world just described. They recalled that they were not permitted to partake of the first fruits of the season (the blueberries, maple sugar, or wild rice) or of the first animal killed until they had made an offering of gratitude to Kijie manido.

As far as we could learn, Kijie manido (usually pronounced Keeshee Munido) is an ancient Algonquian deity. He does not figure significantly in the myths which are now extant. The informants who mentioned Kijie manido evidently thought of him as formal and remote, a deity to be respected and feared, indeed to such an extent that his name was not usually spoken in ordinary conversation.

With Nanabozho, it was otherwise. Here the story tellers felt at home, especially when they related stories of Nana-bozho as a trickster. In these stories Nanabozho is always wandering about. He is always hungry, but he is never permitted to satisfy his hunger. He is always playing tricks on others, though his jokes usually turn on himself. But Nanabozho is not always a trickster. He is an elusive character, as he unites in himself the traits of a god, an animal, and even a human being. He becomes a giver of good. Several of our informants commented on how the Ojibwa were indebted to him for showing them how to use the resources of nature—the maple sugar, wild rice, bass-wood and the birch bark.

But the greatest gift of Nanabozho seems to have been the gift of the Midewiwin (the Mide religion or the Grand Medicine Society). This he bestowed upon the Ojibwa during a time of need, a time of sickness and death.

By means of the Midewiwin, the sick were to be cured and life was to be prolonged, and the knowledge of herbs for such purposes was to be perpetuated. These objectives were to be accomplished through the ceremonies of the society, and thus the teachings of Nanabozho were re-enacted in ritual (the re-enacting of their myths), song, and dance.

Ojibwa mythology is, then, closely associated with the Grand Medicine Society or Mide religion. It is an involved animal mythology. (Myths contained in the Grand Medi-cine Society are given in the appendix for those who are interested in the Mide Society and the old myths of its foundation by Nanabozho.)

Nanabozho as the central figure has counterparts among other Algonquian Indians, but our informants did not mention them. The similarities between Nanabozho and various other mythological characters extend, of course, far beyond the Algonquian family to many North American Indian tribes. The comparisons are impressive. They suggest that here could be one of the doorways to history if adequate records were available.

Our story tellers used different forms for the name of their Ojibwa character. Mainly these forms were: *Nanabozho, Winabozho, Wainabozho,* and on the Nett Lake Reservation, *Nanabushu.* We adopted the first in the list, *Nanabozho,* not because it necessarily represents what we heard most frequently, but rather because we needed to be consistent throughout the book. This form is often used in printed sources, and it seems to be close to the way in which the name was spoken by many, although not all, of the oldest of the Ojibwa we interviewed.

It was not easy to find, at the end of the 1950 decade, the range of Nanabozho episodes that appear in this collection. We searched diligently for good narrators and authentic material. The Nanabozho stories that follow have a broad scope—from Nanabozho's birth and early adventures, his encounter with the evil underwater manidos and the subsequent formation of the new earth, to the lighter trickster and simpleton tales. There is a wide range of characters. Here are to be found Nanabozho's grandmother Nokomis, his brothers, his wife and daughters, Pakiwis, and the many animals. Also, because

59

the Ojibwa like to place their central character in their own everyday world, there are tales wherein Nanabozho becomes concerned about the depletion of nature's resources, about the restrictions of the game warden, about a bank account (however small), and tar paper and nails.

THE BIRTH AND EARLY ADVENTURES OF NANABOZHO

The Ojibwa of northern Minnesota begin their mythology with the birth of Nanabozho. They do not tell about a first creation, although they frequently refer to the new earth that Nanabozho formed later. (This event is related at the end of the myth, "Nanabozho and the Wolves," which begins on page 70.)

In the stories that follow, the two myths in which Nanabozho is specifically designated as a rabbit are placed first. One of them is a version of the birth of the culture hero, and the other tells about the theft of fire. The account of how fire is brought to a people is always an important myth. Therefore we were delighted when in August of 1958, an old story teller on the Fond du Lac Reservation told us how Nanabozho as a rabbit brought fire to the Ojibwa.

After these two myths, there follows a remarkably full narrative called "This Is the Beginning." An Ojibwa woman from the northern part of the Leech Lake Reservation told it to us. She handled the events masterfully, and all the more so if one considers that we came unannounced. Several of the Ojibwa we interviewed knew fragments of the narrative, but here was a story teller who related a continuous myth. She seemed to keep searching

60

for the exact way in which she had heard the events told
to her long ago. Evidence of the fragility of this oral
tradition came to us when a few months later, we heard
that the elderly narrator had died.

Following these accounts, there is the myth of how
Nanabazho brought the gift of corn to the Ojibwa and
then two stories of encounters of Nanabozho with his
brothers. In one of the encounters, the existence of death
is accounted for. An Ojibwa on the Nett Lake Reservation who knew much of the old material told us this myth.
The brother in the story is sent to rule over the land of
the dead, the south. He is still there, according to the
narrator, and Nanabozho today lives in the east, the direction in which he originally made his home with Nokomis.
Since the four cardinal points ("the four corners of the
wind") are important in Ojibwa mythology, the elderly
Indian's comments, as summarized here, are of interest:
There are manidos at each of the four directions. In the
east, the manidos are red. Nanabozho made these. In the
south, they are blue and in the west, yellow. In the north,
where it is so cold that no one ever goes, the manidos are
white. We hear them when we hear the north wind. The
Ojibwa (and here the old man pointed with emphasis and
deliberation) always speak of the directions in this order—
east, south, west, and north.

There is a dignified tone in the narratives that tell about
the birth and early adventures of Nanabozho. The action
takes place at an indeterminable time in a far-distant
mythical age. One episode after another reveals Nanabozho as a powerful supernatural being. He sometimes
seems ruthless, but there is little of the trickster here. In

general, his deeds are on a large scale, they are for a serious purpose, and they are lasting in effect. He brings back fire from a far-away "country." He creates the idea of death, so that there will be enough room on earth, and he establishes a home for the dead. He gives corn to the Indians. He brings many of the animals and fish into existence. Nanabozho is thus portrayed as a force in the development of a pattern in the universe.

NANABOZHO AS RABBIT
NANABOZHO and the RICE BASKET

One day as Nanabozho's grandmother Nokomis was smoking meat on the rack over the fire, a big storm came up. The wind blew hard and tipped over a rice basket that was on the ground. A little rabbit ran from under the basket. Nokomis ran after the rabbit and when she caught it, she recognized her grandson Nanabozho.

* * * *

THE THEFT of FIRE

Some people in the distance—in a far-off country—had fire. The rabbit said that he wanted to get it, and so he went to this country.

He thought, "If I could just steal one of the sparks!"

The people in the distant country let the rabbit lie by the fire. A spark from a piece of wood fell on his back, just as he hoped it would. Then the rabbit ran off with the spark. The people in the far-off country chased him, but he got away from them.

This rabbit was Nanabozho.

THIS IS THE BEGINNING

This is the beginning of the story of Nanabozho. Nanabozho had no mother. He lived with his grandmother. This is how it was . . . .

One day Nanabozho's mother went out with her mother to get wood. After a while, the mother missed her daughter. There was a very high wind. She looked for her daughter, but she could not find her.

Later when the grandmother was chopping wood, she found a little blood on one of the pieces. She brought the piece of wood into the wigwam. She knew the blood was her daughter's. The next morning there was a little baby. That was the beginning of Nanabozho's life, and he lived with his grandmother.

Nanabozho was curious about his parents. So he asked his grandmother. "The four corners of the wind killed your mother," she said.

Then Nanabozho was angry. He wanted to find his mother, but his grandmother said, "No, She was blown to pieces. You can't find her."

So Nanabozho built a canoe of birch bark. "I'm going to find out who killed my mother and why."

He took his canoe out on Lake Superior and he called up a wind. (He had power to talk to everything—animals, trees, wind, and everything.) He remembered that his grandmother had warned him, "There is a powerful man out there that you will never be able to reach. There is a heavy gum on the water and you will never be able to get through it."

But as it turned out, Nanabozho had the power to go

through it, and he finally reached the powerful man. This man knew that Nanabozho was coming after him.

This is true—this is the beginning of the story of Nanabozho that I am telling you.

Then Nanabozho got there, and he said to the man, "I came to see you. We are going to fight." Nanabozho shot at him with his bow and arrow, but he could not kill him. The other man was so powerful.

Nanabozho kicked at a little weasel which was under his foot. The weasel was crying. The weasel said to Nanabozho, "I was going to tell you where to hit—where his life is."

So Nanabozho got hold of the weasel. "Friend," he said," tell me. I will make you beautiful. Tell me how you want to look."

The weasel told Nanabozho that he wanted to be white with a little black here and there—(just the way the weasel looks today). "See that bunch of hair at the back of his neck? That is where he keeps his life," said the weasel.

Nanabozho had only two arrows left. The powerful man dared Nanabozho. "You can hit my body any place. You can't kill me."

Nanabozho and the powerful man chased each other up and down, and they fought hard. Then Nanabozho had only one arrow left and he hit the bunch of hair on the back of the man's neck and killed him.

After that, Nanabozho cut the man up in small pieces. All the small animals came from these pieces—some mean and some good.

Then Nanabozho went home and told his grandmother

what he had done. She said, "You've done something no one else could do."

The next day Nanabozho went in his canoe again. He called for a wind, but there was no wind. Then he called for Mas-ki-no-zha (the Great Pike) to come and swallow him and his canoe. So Mas-ki-no-zha did.

Nanabozho cut Mas-ki-no-zha inside and killed him. Finally the big fish washed ashore and the birds of all kinds started to eat the meat. Nanabozho told the birds to make a hole and help him get out. They did. Then Nanabozho cut up Mas-ki-no-zha and that's where all the small fish come from. Nanabozho went home and told his grandmother.

Now I have told you the beginning of Nanabozho's life.

* * * *

(VARIATIONS, as told by other OJIBWA)

Concerning the birth of Nanabozho, we were told how the brothers argued as to which one would be born first, and while they were quarreling, the mother died. We also learned that it was the birth of Flint that caused the mother's death.

We heard that later Nanabozho set out to find Flint, and Flint was expecting him. One narrator said, "The youngest brother was sharp like a razor. He lived on an island, where he watched for Nanabozho. He was afraid of Nanabozho and knew that he was coming, so he gathered pine pitch and put it in the water all around the island." Here the powerful man is identified as a brother of Nanabozho. Two of the Ojibwa spoke of him as Mudjikiwis.

(We tried to find out all that we could about Mudjikiwis, but we concluded that whatever role this character may once have had in Ojibwa folklore, it has now become confused. Several informants spoke of Mudjikiwis as a powerful thunderbird. As such, he was considered especially awesome and sometimes bad. He was also associated with the westerly direction and occasionally the West Wind.)

TWO ENCOUNTERS OF NANABOZHO AND HIS BROTHERS

NANABOZHO and HIS YOUNG BROTHER

Nanabozho and one of his brothers never got along. They fought, and Nanabozho killed his young brother. Then he blew on him, and his brother came back to life. Nanabozho said, "When people die, they will go to your land. You will be the leader there. If there is no death, the earth will be too full."

So Nanabozho's brother died and went to rule over his land. (This land is in the south.)

Thereafter there are certain rules. People are punished if they do not listen to Nanabozho. And there will be sickness and death. The medicine men are the ones who send the people to Nanabozho's brother's land.

* * * *

NANABOZHO KILLS HIS OLDER BROTHER

Nanabozho had killed one of his brothers. He had another brother, and he wanted to kill him too, so that there would be no one older than he was.

Nanabozho asked his brother, "What will kill you?"

His brother replied, "Why do you ask? What will kill you?"

66

Nanabozho said, "Only a cat-tail. Now tell me, what will kill you?"

His older brother answered, "All right. I'll tell you—a flint arrow, my brother."

"Let's try," said Nanabozho, "and we'll see who will get hurt."

The older brother got out the cat-tails. Nanabozho got out the flint arrows. They started shooting, and Nanabozho killed his older brother.

NANABOZHO AND MANDOMIN

Nanabozho owned a canoe that would sail and turn at his will. When he had grown a little older, his grandmother Nokomis had a dream that there was a tall and strong brave who must be conquered. So she told Nanabozho exactly where to find this brave whose name was Mandomin. She told him to go across the Great Sea.

So Nanabozho sailed away in his canoe until he reached the other shore. He had no difficulty because his canoe knew just where to go. When he arrived on the other side, he had to cross some mountains. Finally he came upon the tall brave wearing robes of green. This was Mandomin.

Mandomin asked Nanabozho who he was and where he was from. So Nanabozho told of his grandmother's dream and that he was to conquer the young brave. They began to wrestle. Many times Nanabozho became very weak, but he could not give up because he must fulfill his mission to conquer Mandomin for the welfare of the Ojibwa.

Finally Nanabozho conquered. When Mandomin saw that he had lost, he spoke to Nanabozho. "Since you are

better ɛ l stronger that I am, I surrender to you. I will
no long be a brave, but I shall be changed into a stalk
of gree corn. I will give myself up to you so that you
can retu n to your people."

Mandomin then taught Nanabozho how he (Mandomin) was to be buried. He first taught him how to
prepare the soil. When the corn came up, it was very
beneficial as food. That is how the Ojibwa got corn to eat.

NANABOZHO FORMS THE NEW EARTH FOR THE INDIANS

This section contains the particularly significant myth
"Nanabozho and the Wolves." Concepts in it are associated with the ceremony of the Midewiwin and with
hieroglyphics on the birchbark scrolls.

At the opening of the story, Nanabozho is going around
on his adventures, and this time he is traveling with a wolf
pack. The main conflict starts when the underwater manidos, in their continuous warfare against Nanabozho, seize
a young wolf. Nanabozho then seeks revenge, and the
conflict intensifies. Towards the end of the story, there
are the earth-diving incidents. Nanabozho thus forms an
immense island—a new land—for the Indians. This was
necessary, since the old one had been destroyed by a flood.

Several of the Ojibwa on different reservations knew
about the flood, the earth-diving, and the testing of the
earth's size. We heard three quite complete accounts of
these events, and several fragmentary references. However, the incidents relating to the formation of the new
earth are part of a long myth, and therefore we felt for-
tunate in hearing the well-organized, traditional, and con-

tinuous narrative that appears here in "Nanabozho and the Wolves."

One detail may need an explanation. Nanabozho kills the chief of the evil underwater monsters or manidos (the king of the lions or the Great Lion). In doing this, he is helped by a bird (a kingfisher), who advises Nanabozho to shoot the lion's shadow. Here it is important to recognize the Ojibwa concept of the shadow as the soul or spirit.

The end of the myth "Nanabozho and the Wolves" marks the end of a span of time, but how long a time it was, is unknown. The full continuity of the events from the birth of Nanabozho through his forming of the new earth is not determined. The new land that Nanabozho made was intended for the Indians. Its formation, therefore, seemed to mark a new order; the old was "the time of Nanabozho and the animals."[1] Hence the special importance of the story "Nanabozho and the Wolves." It is a narrative that cannot be interpreted in the light of everyday thinking, but at almost every turn, we must accept the story's insistence that here is a mythical world in which our imagination can only approximate the concepts of time, space, and proportion.

---

[1]Many of the events in the Nanabozho tales in the succeeding sections of the book evidently happened within the old order, but since the narratives cannot be arranged in a clearly defined sequence, we have grouped them according to content and type.

NANABOZHO and the WOLVES

Nanabozho talked to everything—the trees and the animals. He always had his own way and everybody believed in him.

One day in early spring, Nanabozho went on a hunt with Old Man Timber Wolf and his two sons. When evening came, they looked for a place to sleep. Nanabozho picked out a nice quiet place where there was no wind. But Old Man Wolf and his sons did not like this place. They found a point where the wind blew cold and that is where they all slept.

In the night Nanabozho got cold. Old Man Wolf told his sons to put a blanket over Nanabozho. They put their tails over him, but Nanabozho did not like the tails. He got too warm. Then the wolves took their tails off Nanabozho. Then he was cold again. This went on and on through the night.

The next day they went different ways. Nanabozho and one of the young wolves went off together. That night Nanabozho dreamed that the young wolf—his adopted son—fell into a creek when he was out after game. When Nanabozho woke up, he warned his adopted son always to throw a stick ahead of him across a dry creek. One day the young wolf went after deer and got lost. Nanabozho went on his way down the river, crying and looking for his adopted son. He was afraid that the dream had come true. He looked for ten days and by this time he was starving.

Nanabozho saw a kingfisher in a tree. Nanabozho said, "I am looking for my adopted son."

The kingfisher said, "I saw certain parties going from the beach to the lake."

Nanabozho went down to the beach and changed himself into a stump. All the animals wondered, "Is this truly a stump, or is it Nanabozho?"

First the king lion—me-she-be-zhe—looked the stump all over. Then a big snake wrapped himself around it. When the animals were now sure that it was just a stump, they went to sleep in the warm sun.

The kingfisher said to Nanabozho, "Don't kill the lion's body. Kill his shadow."

Nanabozho shot the shadow of the lion, the king of the water (me-she-be-zhe, or wa-bi-me-she-be-zhe). Then the other animals chased Nanabozho up and down the river.

Nanabozho saw a little frog—a medicine frog. The frog called out, "EEEEE." She sang, "My bells are ringing— my bells are ringing."

Nanabozho asked the frog, "What are you doing?"

"I am looking for Nanabozho because he shot the king of the water."

Nanabozho killed the frog. He got into the frog's skin and began shaking the frog's bells. He tied the rattles to his heels and went on his way until he came to a wigwam. Over the opening, Nanabozho saw the skin of his adopted son and he almost cried. Inside, the wigwam was crowded with those who were there to be healed. Nanabozho saw that the lion, the king of the water, was one of them. No one looked at Nanabozho shaking his medicine rattles. Nanabozho got over to the lion and he pushed the arrow in the lion's side back and forth, and the king of the water died.

Nanabozho tore off the skin of the frog. Then he grabbed his adopted son's skin that had been used as a flap over the opening of the wigwam, and he ran for a raft.

Then the rains began to come, and the water came higher and higher. The animals couldn't see. They had no place to go, so they all came to Nanabozho's raft. Everywhere there was water.

After they had been on the raft for a long time, Nanabozho said, "Who will go down to get more earth?"

First the loon went and he came up almost dead. Nanabozho breathed on him and got him to live.

Then the hell-diver went and he came up almost dead. Nanabozho breathed on him too and got him to live.

Then the beaver tried and the same thing happened.

Finally the muskrat dived and he came up with earth in his paws. He was almost dead, and Nanabozho made him live.

Nanabozho blew on the sand, and it spread and the earth became larger. He sent a fast hawk to fly around the earth to see if it was large enough for them. It was gone ten days and then it returned. When it came back, Nanabozho sent the muskrat down for more earth. Then Nanabozho blew on the sand again and sent out the hawk. Nanabozho did this until the earth was large enough.

Nanabozho made this earth for the Indians.

NANABOZHO AND THE ANIMALS

Each of the adventures of Nanabozho as he went walking about is quite complete in itself. A substantial number are about Nanabozho and the animals.

In the narratives of this section, the bear, the rabbit, and the hell-diver duck are given a new and permanent appearance, and the red willow comes into existence. Kinnickinick is accounted for. The action takes place in the world of Nanabozho and the animals—"a world before this world," one of our story tellers said.

Often the fun in the adventure starts when Nanabozho begs the animals to help him look or act like them. The animals are wary, for they know that Nanabozho is unwilling to follow directions, and yet they seem to be easily persuaded. The story about the woodpecker shows to what extremes the culture hero-trickster will go in imitating the animals. One way or another in these adventures, Nanabozho acts the simpleton. Sometimes there is just a single episode, but in a narrative like "Nanabozho and the Deer Head," one silly predicament leads to another. In speaking of this adventure tale, an Ojibwa woman said, "Nanabozho did such foolish things! Such foolish things!"

The story of the dancing ducks portrays Nanabozho as both foolish and scheming. Everywhere we went we heard references to this tale, but on the White Earth and Fond du Lac Reservations, we were told two particularly good versions. Both are included here.

The two stories at the end of this section do not have the jovial, trickster-type tone of the others. One of them,

"Nanabozho and the Bear's Grease," is evidently a version of the myth of the animals dipped in fat.

The Ojibwa love to tell about Nanabozho and the animals. They like the humor in the many absurdities, and when they were asked for stories, these were often the tales that first came to mind.

NANABOZHO and the DEER HEAD

One time Nanabozho was going along. He killed a deer and butchered it and cooked it all. Then he had a feast by himself. While he was eating, the wind started to blow hard and the trees squeaked.

"Keep quiet! Keep quiet!" Nanabozho said.

The trees rubbed against each other and squeaked and squeaked. They leaned and fell against each other.

Again Nanabozho said, "Keep quiet! Keep quiet!"

The trees kept on squeaking, and Nanabozho got angry. "I'll fix that!"

He thought the trees must be hungry, so he climbed up one of them and invited the trees to eat with him. He gave them all pieces of meat. Then he got his arm stuck between the limbs of the trees, and he could not go any farther.

While he was there, Nanabozho saw a pack of wolves coming along. "Now, brothers," he said, "don't go along the edge of the woods." And right away the wolves began to swoop in and around the trees, and they found the rest of the meat.

The wind came up again. Nanabozho broke loose from the branches and came down from the tree. He found none of the meat left, just the head of the deer. He saw some meat inside the head and tried to get it. He tried to get at it until he got himself stuck. Then with the deer head still on him, he went down the river. He was going to swim across to ask Nokomis to help him get out of the deer head.

Some Indians came along in a canoe and saw Nanabozho swimming across. They shot at him and thought that they had killed a deer. Nanabozho's head popped out and he laughed at the people. Then he started for home.

NANABOZHO and the WOODPECKER

Nanabozho visited his friends, the wild animals. He visited each one and found they had no food in the house. He visited the bear. He visited the woodpecker.

There was nothing to eat in the woodpecker's kettle. "Nanabozho must be hungry." said the woodpecker. "What can we put in the kettle to boil?"

In the center of the wigwam was a dry cedar. Woodpecker flew up the cedar, made a big noise, and pecked and hammered on different parts of the tree. He hammered and out fell a raccoon. Lady Woodpecker put it in the kettle and prepared it for Nanabozho to eat.

Then Nanabozho started out, but he left his mittens in the wigwam. "Hey, Woodpecker, bring me my mittens."

Woodpecker said to his children, "Don't go near him. I'll give him his mittens." Woodpecker gave Nanabozho his mittens.

Nanabozho said, "Come up to my wigwam some time and get dry meat."

A few months later Woodpecker went to visit Nanabozho. There was a big cedar pole inside his home. Nanabozho said, "Old Lady, go and get a kettle. Friend Wood-pecker might be hungry."

Nanabozho got a sharp bone and stuck it in his nose, as Woodpecker did. He slid up and down the pole and hammered and hammered. He pounded so hard that he fell down in a faint. Woodpecker pulled the bone out of Nana-bozho's nose. Then he went home. He got nothing to eat.

NANABOZHO and the DANCING DUCKS
(First Version)

Nanabozho had traveled a long way. He was hungry. On his back he had a bag that belonged to his grand-mother. He came to a lake and made a little wigwam. He filled his old bag with leaves and went down to the shore. He called to some ducks to come closer. "Hey, come here," he said. "I've got something good for you. I've got a bag full of songs from another country—from the south. I've got many good songs—and some new ones. Come to my wigwam and dance."

"No," the ducks thought. "He's tricky." But then any-way they followed him up to the wigwam and started singing. One little fellow stood by the door and wouldn't come in. He was afraid of Nanabozho.

Nanabozho said to the ducks, "Shut your eyes. If you look, you'll have red eye-lids. I'll sing. You dance. Make all the noise you can."

Nanabozho sang:

"My brothers, don't look.
If you look, you'll have red eyes."

Nanabozho got them to make a noise as they danced and he sang. The ducks made a big noise, "Quack, quack!"

76

and the geese, "Honk, Honk!" All the while, Nanabozho danced too and every now and then he would take a duck or goose and wring its neck.

"My brothers, don't look.

If you look, you'll have red eyes."

Finally the little one by the door peeked. Nanabozho ran after him. Nanabozho was so angry that he kicked him in his back and sprained it. The duck was not able to move.

"Lie there," said Nanabozho. "From now on, you'll be called hell-diver or shingebis. And you'll not be able to walk." To this day, the hell-diver's legs are up on his hips and when he swims, he has to paddle sideways.

Nanabozho took what game he had and started out. After a while he gathered some logs to make a fire. He was tired and went to sleep. He was hungry too, so he took some ducks and stuck them in the ground with their feet out. 'When I wake up," he thought, "the ducks will be well baked." Then he went to sleep.

Some Indians were going by and they saw the smoke. They wondered who it might be. "O, I suppose it's Nanabozho," one of them said. "He's all over." Two or three went up to see. "That's Nanabozho. Keep quiet."

Then they saw the feet of the ducks sticking out, well roasted. They pulled at the legs and got all of the ducks out of the ground. They cut off the legs, stuck them back in the ground, and went away with the roasted ducks.

When Nanabozho woke up, the fire was out. 'Anyway," he thought, "I have my ducks roasted and ready to eat."

But when he pulled at the feet, there were no ducks. He had only the feet left.

(Second Version)

One time Nanabozho saw some ducks, geese, and birds on the lake. He sang to them, 'Come on, come on, come on to my wigwam." He gathered them into his wigwam and shut the opening. He sang and sang, and they danced and danced.

Nanabozho sang:

'Keep your eyes closed. Don't peek.

If you peek, you'll get red eyes."

He knew that one duck was peeking. This duck saw Nanabozho grab the dancers and wring their necks. All the time Nanabozho kept on singing. The little duck saw a place to get out of the wigwam, so he ran for it. Nanabozho ran after him. Just as the duck was going to get out, Nanabozho kicked him on the back. Ever since, this duck has a flat narrow back. He is called hell-diver (or shingebis).

Then Nanabozho went to a high place to bake the ducks that he had killed. He made a big fire and put the ducks all around the edge in the coals and went to sleep. Some Indians came along and saw Nanabozho sleeping. One of the Indians took a feather and tickled him to see if he was sound asleep. His body warned him that Indians were near, and he got up to see about his ducks. He found that they were all there, so he went back to sleep. All this time the Indians were watching him. When Nanabozho went to sleep again, they took the ducks out of the fire, broke off the feet of the ducks, and stuck the feet back where the ducks had been.

After a while, Nanabozho woke up. He was expecting a delicious meal, but when he started to pull his ducks out of the fire, he found only the feet. All of his ducks had been stolen from him.

He was so angry that his body had not warned him that he burned himself as he stood by the fire. Then he went into the woods, and his blood rubbed off on the willow sticks. They became red and to this day they are called red willows. The Indians mix the bark of the red willow with tobacco to make kinnickinick (mish-qua-bemish). So this is how the Indians got kinnickinick to smoke.

NANABOZHO and the BEAVER

One time in early winter when the lake was smooth like a looking glass, Nanabozho saw a beaver sliding around on the ice. His tail was sliding with him, making a nice noise, "Tink, tink! Tink, tink!"

"Come here, brother," said Nanabozho.

"Now Nanabozho wants something," Beaver thought.

Nanabozho kept on calling. Finally Nanabozho thought, "I'll go to him."

He did. "Brother, make me look like you look."

"You always ask the impossible."

"Do as I say," said Nanabozho.

"I can't do that. That's hard," said Beaver.

"Make me look like you. I want to make a noise on the ice the way you do. Make me a tail that goes 'Tink, tink! Tink, tink!' "

Finally Beaver gave in. "All right, Nanabozho. I'll make it. But you never do what you're asked to do. Now stoop over."

So Beaver stuck a tail on Nanabozho. "Now you've got

79

a tail. Don't look back and you'll always have a tail." But Beaver knew that Nanabozho would look back.

Soon there was more snow and ice everywhere. Nanabozho went skating and his tail went "Tink, tink! Tink, tink!"

"I'd like to look back," thought Nanabozho. "Maybe if I turn a little.—No, I'd better not."

The more the snow gathered and the thicker the ice became on his tail, the louder grew the "Tink, tink! Tink, tink!"

"I'd like to look back at my tail."

Beaver was laughing at Nanabozho.

"Oh, brother," thought Nanabozho, "I'm going to look back!" And pretty soon he did. He tried flapping his tail, but he couldn't.

* * * *

NANABOZHO and the SNIPE

Nanabozho came upon a snipe jumping from log to log in Lake Superior. He wondered if he could do that too.

"Hey, come over here! Teach me how to do that!"

"No, I can't. This is the way I get my food."

But Nanabozho kept on asking.

"All right," said the snipe. "Get on the log and say what I tell you to say. Say 'Big Sea Water with a hole in it.' Don't say 'Sea closes.' "

Nanabozho did as he was told. But soon he got tired of saying the same thing as he jumped from log to log. He changed his tune to "Sea closes," and he went down between two logs and out of sight.

NANABOZHO and the HOOT OWL

Nanabozho and his grandmother Nokomis lived by a lake. One day Nanabozho said, "I'm going fishing."

Nokomis said, "Sure—go fishing."

Nanabozho caught many fish. The hoot owls were watching him. "How can we get the fish away from Nanabozho? How stingy he is!"

Then Nanabozho went home with a lot of fish, but it was not enough for the winter. So Nokomis said, "You will have to go fishing again. We haven't enough for the winter."

Then Nanabozho went back and fished again, and the hoot owls watched him. "What can we do?" they thought. They wanted some of the fish.

"Let's make a funny noise—whoo-oo-oo." Nanabozho looked around. The noise frightened him. He ran away and left all his fish behind.

When he got home, he said, "Old Lady, Old Lady (Noko, Noko), I heard the manidos."

"Where are your fish?"

"I let the manidos have them."

The hoot owls had all they wanted.

NANABOZHO and the BIRDS

Nanabozho spent much time with the birds and learned their ways by watching them. He talked with the birds and asked them to teach him how to fly.

So the birds taught Nanabozho how to fly, but they said, "Never look down or you will fall."

Nanabozho learned quickly and flew well, but he did not like to do what he was told. As he flew over a village he heard people cheering and calling, "Nanabozho is flying with the birds! Nanabozho is flying with the birds!" Nanabozho looked down and he fell to the ground.

TWO ANIMAL STORIES of a MORE SERIOUS NATURE
NANABOZHO and the BEAR'S GREASE

Nanabozho killed a bear, and Nokomis cut off the fat from the meat. Then Nanabozho got Nokomis to boil the fat and dump it in a hollow. He started singing and called the birds and animals. "Here is a puddle of bear grease. Do whatever you want to do with it. You can swim in it or drink it or take as much as you want of it."

The rabbit came and dipped his paws in the bear grease and put the fat on his neck and shoulders. He said, "I'll only put it on my neck and shoulders, so I won't be too heavy." That is why the rabbit has two strips of fat on his shoulders.

Then a bear came along. Nanabozho said again, "Take as much grease as you want, and that will be as much fat as you will have." The bear swam right across the puddle of fat and so that is the reason the bear is so fat.

* * * *

NANABOZHO and the SNOWSHOE RABBIT

Nanabozho and the snowshoe rabbit were going to have a great feast. The rabbit was supposed to mix the tobacco. He mixed it with his paws and then showed his paws to Nanabozho.

"Look, Nanabozho! My feet are yellow."

Nanabozho answered, "Brother, your feet will now look like this from generation to generation."

82

NANABOZHO AND NATURAL PHENOMENA

THIS SECTION contains stories of the trees, the cranberry bushes, the bulrushes, and the seasons. Some of the incidents from the animal narratives in the preceding section logically belong here as well; particularly the incident about the origin of red willow in "Nanabozho and the Dancing Ducks" and the adventure with the squeaking trees in "Nanabozho and the Deer Head."

The inseparableness of Nanabozho and nature is again apparent. We found the same idea in comments offered apart from the stories. The vines on the trees are Nanabozho's intestines, and the fungus is the mark made by his knees. And in the winter, when the house creaks and thumps, then Nanabozho is bumping his head against the outside walls.

The stories that follow range from the extremely serious mood of "Nanabozho and the Birch Tree" to the lighter or the comic, as in "Nanabozho and the Bulrushes."

NANABOZHO and the BIRCH TREE

The narrator prefaced her story by saying that the birch tree was placed on Indian land for the Indian people. The birch wood, she explained, was good for fires and torches. The bark was used for making baskets necessary in preserving food and in winnowing the wild rice. The bark was also used in making canoes and wigwams and in burying the dead. The Ojibwa, she said, etched their history on birchbark scrolls. They considered the birch trees almost sacred.

Why, then, should the beauty of this highly esteemed

tree be marred? The story simply states that there has been an offense. Is Nanabozho's motive to be found in revenge? In jealousy? Is Nanabozho in the role of a cruel trickster? His act, of course, accounts for the markings on birch bark today. One Ojibwa (not the teller of the story that follows) saved a piece of bark over a period of several months, so that on our next visit, he could show us how the spread of a bird's wing is clearly outlined.

*　*　*　*

The birch tree used to be very tall, sleek, white, and unmarred except for where the branches grew out of its side.

Nanabozho's struggles were always many. One day he encountered the birch tree. The tree had committed some terrible offense for which it had to be punished. So Nanabozho cursed the birch tree.

He took a bird and banged it against the birch tree. He banged and whacked it on this side and that. This is why the birch tree today is badly marred. The marks on the birch tree look like wings spread out. Nanabozho said, "Hereafter this is the way you will look."

That is all.

*　*　*　*

NANABOZHO and the PINE TREE

Nanabozho's desire to be like nature sometimes led him into stupid situations, as in the story that follows. However, the elderly narrator did not seem to think this stupidity at all incongruous with other stories that revealed the culture hero's power over nature.

*　*　*　*

Nanabozho was going along the lake shore. He came

84

to a hollow pine tree with a big limb hanging out over the lake. The tree was singing in the wind. The wind would go in one knot hole and out another.

Nanabozho called to the tree, "Young brother, what are you doing? Will you make me like that?"

The tree didn't care to. It said, "I must stay this way," and it kept on singing.

Nanabozho still bothered the tree. Finally it said, "Well all right, crawl up here. Do you see this hollow? Put your arm in there. Now say what I say, 'I'm pointing out to the lake.' You say that too."

Nanabozho did as the pine tree told him. He got stuck in the hollow of the tree and had to stay there all day and all night. He got tired and hungry.

The next day a big wind storm came along and blew the tree down. Then Nanabozho got out.

TWO SHORT ACCOUNTS of NANABOZHO as SIMPLETON
NANABOZHO and the CRANBERRIES

One day Nanabozho was walking along the edge of a lake. The water was like a looking glass. In the water he saw some berries. He said, "I am going to get them and eat all I want."

Nanabozho reached for the berries. He fell into the water and bumped his head hard against a rock. He came out crying and rubbing his head. While he was sitting on the shore, he turned his head and saw high-bush cranberry bushes above him. Nanabozho had been diving at their shadows.

NANABOZHO and the BULRUSHES

One night Nanabozho was traveling along. He saw people dancing and he went over to where they were. All night long he danced. Then in the morning, the wind went down, and Nanabozho saw that he had been dancing with the bulrushes.

NANABOZHO and WINTER-MAKER

Merciless Winter-Maker acknowledges his defeat for the time being, but he is not destroyed. He will return.

It is Nanabozho who stirs up discontent among the Ojibwa. Although he is partly the trickster in this story, he is still more the culture hero who acts for the good of the Indians. The outcome suggests that winter and summer are being established as seasons.

* * * *

Once upon a time this country was a big glacier. It was all ice and never was summer. The Indians lived here. They lived on and on.

One day Nanabozho came along. He said to the Indians, "How are you going to keep on living in this snow and ice? There must be something we can do to make it more productive." Nanabozho stirred them up.

The Indians then meditated. They made sacrifices and offerings, and fasted and prayed to the Great Spirit. They kept on meditating. They did not know what to do. They had been living comfortably before.

This problem was so great that they assembled again. They invited Nanabozho to sit in council at a feast to see what they could do about the great fear. When they were assembled, one old Indian, the wisest of the Ojibwa, said,

86

"There is only one thing we can do. We shall have a feast of wild rice and wild roots and invite Old Man Winter— the Winter-Maker— to it. Nanabozho will be our scout. He knows where Old Man Winter is." Nanabozho then prepared tobacco to take along to invite Old Winter-Maker to the feast.

Before the council began, the Indians huddled in secret. They planned to feed Old Man Winter a feast of boiling hot rice and herbs. They planned to keep him there and give him hotter and hotter food, so that he would grow fatter and sleepy, and sweat.

Finally Old Man Winter came. Oh, how the cold came when he came! Everything grew cold. The trees cracked and the forests cracked. The Indians kept on making the food hotter with hotter and hotter coals. Old Man Winter kept on eating and eating and growing warmer and warmer and perspiring more and more. At last, Old Man Winter said, "You've got me. I believe I'll go."

He walked out into the north and disappeared. When the Indians looked out, they saw green grass and fields and fruit trees and birds. But they heard Old Winter-Maker calling, "I'm coming back; I'm coming back!"

PAKIWIS AND NANABOZHO

W HO WAS Pakiwis? (Pronounced Pak-i-wis, with the first and last syllables usually given a sharp accent.) We kept searching for information about him, and for a while it seemed as if we were looking for the impossible. Finally on the Fond du Lac Reservation, we heard this: "They say he runs in February." Soon we heard that Pakiwis and Nanabozho were often on opposite sides. If Nanabozho let the Indians have a warm January, then Pakiwis would surely see that they had a cold February. We noted that it was only the oldest of our informants who were able to comment on Pakiwis. Four of them believed that Pakiwis and Mudjikiwis were brothers of Nanabozho, but others considered this relationship vague. On one of our trips back to the Nett Lake Reservation, we heard that Pakiwis was the partridge in the world of Nanabozho and the animals before the formation of the new earth.

At last we were told the Pakiwis narratives that follow —"The March Whirlwind" and two accounts about the Pakiwis and Nanabozho families. There are similarities in the three narratives: The main conflict in each centers on fish (or food), and Nanabozho and Pakiwis play the role of opposites.

We were informed that the story of "The March Whirlwind" was also sometimes told so that it was Pakiwis who lost his fish, and not Nanabozho. Another very short account that we heard on the Fond du Lac Reservation makes Pakiwis the target of much laughter: Pakiwis was going around with a bag of fish. He tried to join some young men who were out ice fishing, but he was not wanted. As he ran back to shore on the ice, he fell into one pot hole after another and lost his bag of fish to the fellows who were laughing at him all the time.

*   *   *   *

THE MARCH WHIRLWIND

Would that we could reproduce the story teller's accompanying dramatization, especially in the two scenes where the spirits hit, shove, and chase!

* * * *

The families of Nanabozho and Pakiwis had no food, and so Pakiwis went out to look for some. He heard the spirits talking to him. "Go to where the ice is piled high and fill your bag full of ice and snow. No matter what happens, you must not turn around and look back. When you come to a pond in a hollow, put your bag down and leave it."

Pakiwis did that. He filled his bag with ice and snow and as he walked along, the spirits hit him and shoved him and chased him, or so he thought, but it was the March wind blowing. The next morning Pakiwis went back to the hollow and there he found his bag full of fish.

On the way home he met Nanabozho. Nanabozho said, "Where did you get all those fish?"

"I got them over there in the hollow," Pakiwis said. Then he told Nanabozho how he could get some too.

So Nanabozho went to where the ice was piled high and filled his bag with ice and snow. Then as he walked along, the spirits hit him and shoved him and chased him. Nanabozho heard voices saying, "Here is Nanabozho! Here is Nanabozho! Let's chase him."

It was only the March whirlwind, but Nanabozho could not stand it any longer and he looked back. He left his bag in the hollow. The next morning he came for his fish, but he had none.

89

THE FAMILIES of PAKIWIS and NANABOZHO

The two accounts that follow were related by very old Indians living on different reservations. The first narrator was ninety years of age, and the second (who spoke only in Ojibwa) was almost a hundred. Both seemed to enjoy themselves thoroughly as they told the stories.

* * * *

(First Account)

Pakiwis and Nanabozho had gathered their food in the fall. (Nanabozho was lazy, but this time he was different.)

"We'll eat your food first," Nanabozho said.

"All right," Pakiwis said (just so there would be no trouble).

In the spring, Pakiwis' food was all eaten up. One day when Pakiwis and Nanabozho were going out to fish, Nanabozho said to his wife, "Make trouble with Pakiwis' wife. Make trouble."

So she did, and when Pakiwis and Nanabozho came home, the women were quarreling.

Nanabozho's wife said, "Did you tell Pakiwis that you told me to make—?"

"Keep quiet! Keep quiet!" said Nanabozho.

* * * *

(Second Account)

One time the families of Pakiwis and Nanabozho lived together. They ate up Pakiwis' fish first. Then Nanabozho moved and took his fish with him. So Pakiwis' family had no fish to eat, and they went hungry.

NANABOZHO BURIES HIS GRANDMOTHER

 T HE GRANDMOTHER is an important figure in Ojibwa life and story. Nanabozho lived with his grandmother Nokomis during his childhood and youth. There was often much joking and bickering between the two, but when Nokomis died, Nanabozho buried her with all due respect. According to the story that follows, he observed the tradition of wrapping the body in birch bark, and he planted a cedar near the grave. Thus the birch and the cedar—both significant trees to the Ojibwa—entered into the burial and commemoration of Nokomis.

At times, Nokomis has been referred to as the earth (or mother earth), but we found little support for this concept. The general interpretation among the Ojibwa we interviewed seemed to be that Nokomis is simply *grandmother*. There was one who was older than Nokomis, we were told. An Ojibwa said that Me-suk-kum-wik-o-kwe is the earth. Another woman commented that all Indians have one mother, and she is the earth, but this is not Nokomis. The same informant went on to explain that the early Indians never picked a cranberry or blueberry patch "clean," because something must be left for the earth.

Nokomis as grandmother is still close to many of the older Ojibwa on northern Minnesota reservations. The story tellers spoke affectionately of her, and they liked to call her "Noko" or "Old Lady."

* * * *

One day when Nanabozho came home he found that his old lady, his grandmother Nokomis, had died. Her wigwam was down in a ravine where the wind did not strike too much.

Nanabozho climbed a high rocky hill between Grand Portage and Grand Marais. (Nanabozho's footprints can still be seen on this hill.) He wrapped his grandmother in birch bark and buried her. Then he thought that some day he would be going by there and he would not know where to find Nokomis' grave, so he said to himself, "I will plant a cedar right near Old Lady's head."

Some years later he came back to the spot. He looked to see if Old Lady was still there. He found a cedar six to eight feet high. Then he dug at the roots of the cedar and he found that they had grown around Old Lady's forehead.

NANABOZHO IN DISGRACE

Rarely does one find a stronger picture of shame and defeat than that which ends a folk tale recorded on the Red Lake Reservation in 1911 by de Josselin de Jong, who came from Europe to study the Ojibwa language: Nanabozho goes from place to place. He asks the boys in the village, "What is the news?" They answer that there is nothing except that Nanabozho marries his daughters. He comes to another village, and asks again, 'What is the news?" And again he receives the same answer. Nanabozho is sure then that all of the people have heard. He looks for a tall tree and climbs to the very top, hoping to have the gossip blown away by the wind. But at the top of the tree, he still hears the news of his disgrace. Nanabozho could do or be anything he wished, but he was not able to have this news blown away, for incest was a violation of a cultural taboo of the Ojibwa (and also of other North American Indians).

We heard this story frequently referred to on all of the northern Minnesota reservations, and we were told four well-organized versions. Two of the versions are included here. Each is different from the other, and yet both follow the general pattern of the narrative as it has been recorded among various North American Indian tribes: The trickster gives instructions to his family and then pretends death, he comes back and marries his daughter, and he is eventually identified and in disgrace. Sometimes, as the story is told by North American Indians, Nanabozho marries both of his daughters, and sometimes the relationship of the girl is that of stepdaughter, sister, or niece. The trickster varies according to the region—Nanabozho, Coyote, Iktomi, or others. The story has also been reported from Indians of southern South America. The "news" is both widespread and persistent.

* * * *

NANABOZHO MARRIES HIS OWN DAUGHTER
(First Version)

Nanabozho was a widower. He had two girls and a boy. He told his daughters, "Never refuse a man who asks to marry you."

After a while he made believe he was dead. They buried him and put things out on his grave for him to eat.

Later he came back, but they did not recognize him. He married the oldest daughter.

One day Nanabozho and his boy went out hunting beaver. Nanabozho boasted and called the boy "son and brother-in-law."

93

When they returned from the hunt, the boy asked his sister, "Why does he call me son and brother-in-law?"

The sisters wondered. They decided to look for a scar which their father had on his head. They knew that their father had a certain scar. When Nanabozho was sleeping, the girls found it. Then they ran away and left Nanabozho.

Nanabozho did not know what to do, so he started traveling. He went from village to village. He asked little children, 'Have you heard anything about Nanabozho?"

"Yes," they answered, "we heard that Nanabozho married his own daughter."

Everybody semed to know of his shame and so he kept on going. No one knows what became of him.

* * * *

(Second Version)

Nanabozho got sick and was dying. "If I should die," he said to his daughter, "bury me over in that hollow and put a few sticks over me. In case a stranger should come here after I die, his name will be Nahnuh. You should marry him if he comes."

Nanabozho held his breath and made believe that he was dead. He was kept a few days and tested if dead or alive. His sons were a little suspicious. They buried him over in the hollow and covered his grave with brush. For three days, the girls brought food for him and built a fire near his grave. After three days, the girls did not come any more.

Then Nanabozho crawled out of his grave and went to another country. No one knows where. He changed his appearance. He painted his face and dressed up like a young man. He tied skunk hides on his legs.

94

One of the sons saw him first. The son told the mother and she asked the stranger, "Is your name Nahnuh?" She remembered that Nanabozho had said that a stranger might come named Nahnuh and that the daughter should marry him.

Nanabozho stayed on as a stranger. He fooled the old lady and the daughter too, and married the daughter.

In the spring, he and his two sons went to a certain place to fish. Nanabozho was not having any luck. He got excited and said, "My son! Excuse me—my brother-in-law." The older son became suspicious.

When they reached home, the son told his mother what had happened. The old lady felt that there was something strange about this and so she told her daughter.

"Are there any marks that would tell us?" the daughter asked.

"Yes," the mother said. "Once when Nanabozho was out ice-fishing, he had to hang on to a log to save himself, and the ice cut him on the head and left scars. Rub your husband's head until he falls asleep and then look to see if you can find these scars."

The daughter did this, and the old lady found out that the stranger was Nanabozho. She beat him up with a stick and drove him out.

Nanabozho never came back to his family again.

* * * *

(Variations)

The following incident in a version told to us at Fond du Lac gives a variation in the scene in which Nanabozho makes his son suspicious:

One day Nanabozho and his son were hunting in the

woods. Nanabozho got excited when a squirrel—or deer—
went by, and he called out his son's "real name."

"Ah-che-dah-mo!" Nanabozho called. (*Ah-che-dah-mo*
means squirrel.) Then the son started to wonder who the
"stranger" was.

* * * *

We shall begin the narrative that we heard on the White
Earth Reservation with the events coming immediately
after Nanabozho's identity has been revealed:

"I'm glad I didn't marry him," the other sister said.

Both of the girls felt awful. They cried and ran outside.
The younger one knew many tricks. She saw a pile of
wood to be chopped, and she said, "Ax, ax! Chop, chop!
Keep chopping!"

After a while Nanabozho woke up. "Why are those
women chopping so much wood? Are they crazy?"

He put a blanket over himself and away he went to the
woodpile, but there were no women in sight.

Then he started out and he came to a village. As he
went along, he asked, "Have you seen any women? Did
they spread any news?"

MODERN TALES ABOUT NANABOZHO

Nanabozho is not pervasively thought of
as ending his days in disgrace, in spite of the fact that this
idea might seem to be suggested by the story in the preceding section. To some of our informants, he is said to
be continuing in his habit of walking about, though not
necessarily under the shadow of a grave misdeed. At Nett
Lake, we heard that Nanabozho still lives in his home

in the east and that he lives with his grandmother. At
Fond du Lac, we heard that he is living out on an island
somewhere. At Grand Portage, we heard that he is the
sleeping giant (a rock formation) in Thunder Bay farther
up the north shore of Lake Superior, near Fort William-
Port Arthur, Canada.

Other Ojibwa told us tales of Nanabozho as a character
in modern life. The narrators of the first two stories that
follow had great fun projecting the traditional figure into
their own experiences. They interrupted their stories with
laughter as they thought of the incongruities in the situations—Nanabozho having to go to town to buy the where-
withal to finish his house, or being restricted in his hunting
or fishing (evidently outside the reservation land). A
third narrator, in more formal style, told a tale that reflects
pride in the Ojibwa culture hero. It is not surprising that
Nanabozho and Paul Bunyan should come into conflict.
The two folk characters were too different for it to be
otherwise and so also were the worlds they represented.
Paul Bunyan's world reflects a modern economy and a
modern mood. His is the world of organized industrial
enterprise; Nanabozho's is much more the unencumbered
world of nature.

NANABOZHO BUILDS A HOUSE

Once upon a time Nanabozho lived at Buck Lake. He
got tired of living in a wigwam, so he thought that he'd
make a log house. One day he went to the woods to cut
down trees. He worked for a long time. He used horses
to pull down the trees and haul the logs to the place.
Finally he had enough to build his house. When he was

97

nearly finished, he made holes for the doors and windows.

Nanabozho did all that. Then he said, 'Old Lady—Noko—we've got no tar paper, and we've got no nails—we'll have to go to Cass Lake."

* * * *

NANABOZHO and the WPA

It was during the depression. The Indians were having a council meeting at Cass Lake, and they were making no headway. One of them decided to take a walk. He met Nanabozho.

Nanabozho said, "You look sad, my son."

"Yes, I am. We are having a meeting to settle things for the Indians. But we don't get anywhere. Our funds are low and we're going to run out of money."

Then Nanabozho spoke. "You're not the only one who's puzzled. Long ago there was plenty of deer. There was enough meat for food, hides for clothing, sinew for thread, hoofs for little baskets. I used to soak the brains and rub them on the deer hide to soften it. I hung up the deer hide on racks before a slow fire to dry it. I cut up the deer meat and put it in a clean cloth sack and then later I used it for making soup. I sliced it and chopped it fine for soup and other dishes.

"Now I can't do this. There are game wardens. The new laws affect me too. I go fishing and turn around, and the game warden tells me I'm over my limit. I want rabbit and I set my snares, and the game warden tells me I can't do that either.

"My brother, I am troubled. But I feel sorry for you. I have two dollars in the bank. You can have it." (Imagine Nanabozho having money in the bank.)

"Long ago," Nanabozho said, "I controlled everything. Now there are big officials. Tell me how to get on WPA."

* * * *

NANABOZHO and PAUL BUNYAN

The Indians lived in a wooded country. Paul Bunyan came and started logging. The Indians gave a distress signal. The partridges took up the signal and began drumming. They passed the signal on to the loons, and then the loons gave out their cry. All of the animals of the air and the woods joined in passing on the signal. The bears roared, the wild cats screeched, the ducks quacked, the geese honked. The signal came like a wave to Nanabozho, who was two hundred miles away, down by the St. Croix River. Immediately he hustled to save the Indians' land.

Another signal went out that Nanabozho was on his way. "Nanabozho is coming! Nanabozho is coming!"

The waves of sound traveled faster than he could. On the way he met Paul Bunyan. They argued and fought for three days about cutting the trees.

Nanabozho said, "The trees are god-given. The Indians and the animals need them."

That there are pine trees today in Minnesota is proof that Nanabozho won out.

PART III

NOTES ON THE THUNDERBIRD

From near the family wigwam on Minnesota Point, an Ojibwa lad of the 1880's watched the storm clouds gather over the steep dark hills that line the north shore of Lake Superior. When the thunder clapped, the boy's mother explained, "That is the animikig striking their wings against the hills." And when the lightning cut zigzag lines across the sky, she said, 'That is the flashing of the animikig's eyes."

The mother was instilling in her son Ojibwa beliefs concerning the animikig—the thunderbirds. The strength of such beliefs is illustrated by a comment that we heard an old Indian of northern Minnesota make in 1958: "The thunder is not made by clouds bumping against each other. It is the animikig."

Heat lightning is also accounted for in this mythological concept. On the reservations at Fond du Lac and White Earth, we were told the story of the young thunderbird who struck the side of a hill and broke his wing. He was then caught between the precipices. When he tried to free himself, he kept on striking against the rocks, and he repeatedly broke his wing as he did so. This explains the continuous flash of heat lightning.

In the Ojibwa tradition, the animikig were classed as great manidos. Some of our informants said that there were four of these thunderbird manidos, while others referred to four leaders and their families. Two of the leaders were thought to be good and the other two bad. Sometimes, although not usually, we heard that there was just one immense thunderbird. Occasionally we heard other terms used—"the thunderers," "the grandfathers," "the old men," or "the old men with wings." "Old Man Thunder is around the wrong time of the year," is a comment that the Ojibwa were likely to make when a thunderstorm came out of season.

The animikig were associated with the four cardinal directions, and they were said to control the four winds. To the Ojibwa, *four* was a sacred or magic number that figured prominently in their ceremonies.

Earlier in the book, we explained how the good thunderbirds aided Nanabozho in the warfare against evil underwater manidos. This theme was a significant part of the Ojibwa religious beliefs. Thunderbird designs were worked on the sacred (or Mide) drum and on ceremonial nettle fiber bags. At the Cass Lake museum when a curator who was not of the Indian race displayed a band having a thunderbird design embroidered on it, the Ojibwa requested the removal of the sacred article.

Our old informants said that they were brought up to regard the thunderbirds with awe and reverence. They were warned "never to speak carelessly about the manidos that bring the rain." Several referred to the custom of appeasing the thunderbirds with tobacco which they placed around the trees or on the water. An Ojibwa woman told how she used to canoe across Leech Lake with her grandmother to pick blueberries on an island some distance away. One afternoon a storm arose. The two berry pickers waited under the shelter of the trees as long as they could and then the grandmother threw tobacco on the water and prayed to the thunderbirds to pass quietly over the lake, so that she and her granddaughter might have a safe journey back to their village. It is no wonder that when the first airplane flew over Red Lake, some of the Ojibwa thought that it was a thunderbird and ran down to the shore with tobacco and cloth as an offering for protection.

An Ojibwa mother told us that four of her children had been named by a person who had dreamed of the animikig. According to tradition, such dreams imparted mystic power to the child. The four ceremonial names that were given in this instance were: Thunder Coming from the West, Bird Going Around in the Air, Bird That Dips Up and Down, and Ice Bird. This little mother has a niche in a broad sweep of time and place, for the concept of the thunderbird is both old and widespread. It has been found among many American Indian tribes and in Asia.

NATURE LORE, MAGIC PRACTICES, AND OMENS

The material that follows does not necessarily represent current beliefs or practices, but it does indicate that at the end of the 1950's, a knowledge about the traditional nature lore, magic practices, and omens still existed on northern Minnesota reservations. Some of the statements have an added significance if one realizes that in the Ojibwa view of life, the natural and the supernatural were closely related and in many ways identical.

Weather Lore

The Ojibwa were dependent upon their natural environment for food, and therefore they watched closely for predictions as to the kind of winter that lay ahead of them. They were interested in noting the time when the geese migrated or when the squirrels stored their acorns, and they generally made comparisons with other years. They observed whether or not the muskrats built large houses or built them close to shore, for these were signs of a severe winter, and it was necessary to have enough food on hand.

The Ojibwa also studied the sky for predictions of cold weather. If "a certain three stars stayed close together to keep warm," or if the sun went down in a brilliant red, then the weather would turn much colder. Concerning the red sunset, one Ojibwa said, "The sun is making a fire to keep himself warm." Another said, "Sometimes at sunset it looks as if a bird has flown through and spread the cloud. In between the layers of cloud, there is the gold or fire of a bird's tail—a pheasant's tail. When this happens in late fall or winter, the next day will be very cold."

After months of winter weather, a strong March wind

was especially welcome as a harbinger of spring. Several of the Ojibwa we interviewed associated Mudjikiwis with spring and rain. These are comments we heard: "Mudjikiwis never used to be around when it was cold."—"It always used to rain where Mudjikiwis was."—"When the March wind goes in circles, Mudjikiwis is running around. Spring is coming closer."

Storms figure prominently in the weather lore of the Ojibwa. There was concern if the sun went down in a cloud or if the moon appeared in the sky like a powder horn. A wolf howling about the wigwam, heat lightning in the southeast, a dream about a thunderbird, all foretold storms. The Indians observed the birds in the forest and around the wigwam for signs of a storm, and here again we find support for a statement that we heard over and over, "Birds meant much to the early Ojibwa." The weather was considered threatening if the owl called all night, and if the yellow hammer, the turtle dove, or the crow perched upon a tree top.

It was also thought that there would be a storm if the chickadee did not finish the last note or syllable of his song. A ninety-year old Ojibwa sang the "Paddle Song," which he said his people used to sing to represent the chickadee, and he pantomimed the paddling of a canoe according to the rhythm:

> Gi ga be
> Gi ga be
> Gi ga me

It was when the chickadee sang the song like this, that there would be a storm:

> Gi ga be

Gi ga be

Gi ga

Stars were important guides in predicting storms and in fact, weather conditions in general. The Ojibwa read the heavens and judged the weather accordingly. The stars helped them in their planting and harvesting and in avoiding needless risks on their canoe journeys. The Ojibwa also determined the directions or the four cardinal points according to the stars, with the North Star as the center.

To avert storms, parents warned their children not to engage in certain activities: Not to make a snow man; not to make whistles by blowing on blades of grass; not to crack holes on the basswood leaves with their breath, and not to play certain games, such as the bull roarer or buzzer. (Bull roarers or buzzers are flat pieces of wood suspended by a string. When whirled, they give a roaring sound.)

Should storms occur, charms were used for protection. Children were encouraged to look for a stone near a tree that had been struck by lightning. This stone was always to be carried as a charm.

Hunting Lore

The Ojibwa hunter relied on observation, experience, and magic. For luring deer, he used the crushed roots of asters. These were said to smell like the animal's hoof. The hunter either smoked the roots or placed them in traps. To snare rabbits, he used the embryo of the animal as magic bait. Other charms that were carried by the hunter were the beaver head and miniature representations of animals into which magic potions had been shot. This magic "hunting medicine"—a mixture of certain crushed

106

roots and vermilion paint—was prepared by the medicine man.

There were omens which the Ojibwa believed brought bad luck in hunting and fishing: To meet an owl or fox on the way, to place guns near the fishing nets, to have a woman touch a bow or gun. It was a sign of bad luck or even of death if nothing was killed in the hunt. It was said that then the animals saw the Indian's spirit in mourning, and fled.

In times of famine, the Ojibwa felt a need of additional power to obtain game. Then the medicine man was called upon for special help. Mide songs were sung, and hunting medicine was applied to the shoulders and arms of the hunters.

Medicine Lore

The Ojibwa were well acquainted with the roots, herbs, and barks that could be used for teas, poultices, ointments, or charms in curing disease or correcting disfigurement. Some of their therapeutic and medical techniques were based on common sense knowledge and experience. Some were part of the Ojibwa beliefs in magic and in the spirit power attained by means of the Mide religion. In the latter, songs and incantations figured prominently in the cure, as did also the rattle, drum, and medicine sack. There were also the techniques used by medicine men or shamans outside the direct province of the Mide society. These practitioners effected cures individually by means of practical psychology and sleight-of-hand performances. A common method was the swallowing and regurgitating of small bones. In this manner, the evil spirits causing the sickness were thought to be driven out.

107

Another common method for curing was the "shaking tent" ceremony performed by the djasakid, commonly called a juggler, a diviner, or a sorcerer. Our informants gave us vivid descriptions of the djasakid's barrel-shaped lodge or cage and his spectacular exhibitions in calling on the different animal spirits. Turtle, whose importance we commented on earlier in introducing the Old Turtle stories, acted as a messenger to receive the answers to questions concerning the cure of the patient. A particularly impressive part of the exhibition was the violent shaking of the lodge. When all was quiet, the djasakid freed himself from the ropes that bound him. He appeared outside the lodge and announced the cure for the patient.

The following is an account of a shaking-tent ceremony as witnessed by one of our informants:

"When I was a young boy, my family lived near Mora, Minnesota, in an Indian village of about 400 people. At one time all of the children were afflicted with scabbies. The parents tried every remedy they knew of to cure the children. They even tried remedies suggested by the lumberjacks in the camp across the river—sulphur and molasses, and wagon wheel grease. But all of these failed, and the scabbies continued to spread. Finally the Indians resorted to the djasakid. I remember watching the men place eight ironwood saplings firmly into the ground in the shape of a circle. They laced small branches between the saplings and covered the entire frame with a blanket. This small lodge or cage was about four feet wide and eight feet high.

"The djasakid entered the lodge after the men had bound him with the ropes. I remember hearing voices within the lodge and seeing the lodge shake from side to side. This meant that the spirits were approaching.

"An old man near the lodge spoke for the Indians. He said, 'Our children are sick with scabbies. We have tried all the medicines of the Indian and the white man, but we cannot cure our children. Now the old people are getting sick, and they will die.'

"Then the tent came to a stop, and the djasakid answered, 'Don't be afraid. Elect two men to be your scouts. Have them make a strawman and set it up in the village. They must wear moccasins, paint their faces, and wear feathers on their heads. Let them shoot until the strawman burns to ashes.'

"The next morning as I was running down to the dam to get fish for breakfast, I saw the scouts carrying the strawman over the hill. They brought it to the center of the village. Then I saw the scouts running back and forth, shouting and shooting. Soon the strawman was only ashes, and not long after, the scabbies were gone."

The Ojibwa also believed in the use of various kinds of charms in curing the sick. This kind of practice was taught in the advanced degrees of the Mide society. Sometimes medicine was applied to a miniature charm or figurine representing the person to be cured. Often drawings of the person were made on the ground, and medicine was applied to these drawings. A queer-shaped stone was another kind of charm. Near it was erected a medicine pole on the end of which were fastened feathers of different colors. The sick could be brought to this stone for cure. Blankets, tobacco, and other gifts were placed at the foot of the pole as compensation to the owner of the stone.

Like many other people, the Ojibwa were interested in cures for warts. These are some of the ingenious methods used: Applying the heart of a wren, canary, or bluebird to the wart while the flesh of the bird was still warm; tying a horsehair around the wart or rubbing the wart with a bone found sticking out of the ground and afterwards returning the bone to the place where it was found; applying grease to the wart and then burying the grease; rubbing the tail of a duck on the wart and then burning the duck's tail.

Protective Charms of Infants

Infant charms were of several kinds. Small round nets (representing spider webs) made of fibers and in later years of yarn were fastened to the hoop of the cradle board to catch the evil in its meshes before it reached the child. A piece of the umbilical cord of girl babies was hung on a tree, so that when the girl grew up, she would be able to chop wood well. A piece of the boy's umbilical cord was placed on the hunting trail or in a bear's den to make sure that the boy would be a good hunter. For either boy or girl, care had to be taken not to place the umbilical cord in the ashes, or the child would burn. Another type of charm was used to ensure the infant's growth. The parents made holes in their child's moccasins to let the spirits know that a new pair soon would be needed.

Love Charms

The most popular type of love charm consisted of wooden or cloth figurines, about an inch or two in height, representing a man and a woman. Some of our informants believed that to be effective the figurines must be made of cedar. The charms were customarily tied together with a thread from the clothing of the desired person. Love medicine—a mixture of powdered herbs, paint, and sometimes tobacco—was attached to or injected into the figurines, which were carried in a small buckskin bag. Sometimes a bag contained the love potion only, without the figurines.

An incident related by an informant showed confidence in the effectiveness of love charms. A young man gave a girl a buckskin bag with the request that she wear it on her clothing, but he warned her not to look inside the bag. This warning worked on the curiosity of the young lady. She was afraid to open the bag, and yet she was most eager to know the contents, so she thought constantly of the young man until finally this interest turned into love.

Sometimes there was need for a counter love charm. An Ojibwa told us that on an occasion he was given a buckskin bag by a young woman. When he realized that this bag contained a love potion, he became worried because he was not interested in the affections of the giver. He therefore purchased an antidote from the medicine woman. The ingredients of the counter charm were known only to the medicine practitioner.

Another incident in which an antidote was used was related to us by an elderly woman who wanted her daughter to discontinue her friendship for a certain young man. The mother poured a counter love potion on a hot stone and had her daughter inhale the fumes. The treatment had no effect. The mother explained that her daughter must have held her nose while the medicine was being applied.

111

Charms for Good Fortune

In early days, the Ojibwa had great faith in the rabbit embryo. Men and women wore rabbit embryos, or carried them in their medicine sacks, as charms to bring good fortune, The finding of an embryo was considered of such importance that frequently a feast was given to celebrate the occasion.

Evil Magic

It was in the power of those who worked magic to do good or evil. Our informants held the early medicine man in awe. They recounted instances in which relatives or friends had become partially paralyzed or had even met death through the effects of evil potions or magic spells.

Omens

Sometimes seemingly inconsequential personal reactions were considered omens: If an Indian felt a touch on his shoulder, it meant that someone was coming to visit him or that his pack would be filled with game. If his mouth shook, it signified that he was going to cry, or hear bad news. If his chin quivered, it was a sign that he would eat grease or fat meat. If his leg jerked, it was predicted that he would be killed, or that he would have to run for his life, or that he would go on a journey, or that he would go hunting. If his upper lip twitched, it meant that he would lose his temper or that he would be frightened. If his eye twitched, it meant that he would have a pleasant surprise, or that he would see some one, or that he would cry.

We also heard these omens: A person who sees a place where a mole has burrowed under the ground will meet misfortune. A member of his family will die. It is bad luck to return to the wigwam for something that has been forgotten. Some of the Ojibwa said that they would return, but only after they had first sat down and smoked.

APPENDIX

The Mide (Grand Medicine) Society As It Was Practiced by Northern Minnesota Ojibwa.

Sister Bernard Coleman, *Decorative Designs of the Ojibwa of Northern Minnesota* (Washington, D. C.: Catholic University of America Press, 1947); Sister Bernard Coleman, "The Religion of the Ojibwa of Northern Minnesota," *Primitive Man,* 10: 1-25 (1937); Frances Densmore, *Chippewa Customs,* Bureau of American Ethnology Bulletin 86 (Washington, D. C.: Government Printing Office, 1929); Frances Densmore, *Chippewa Music,* Bureau of American Ethnology Bulletin 45 (Washington, D. C.: Government Printing Office, 1910); W. J. Hoffman, "The Midewiwin or 'Grand Medicine Society' of the Ojibwa," in *Seventh Annual Report of the Bureau of American Ethnology,* (Washington, D. C.: Government Printing Office, 1891), 149-300; William Jones, OT, II; William W. Warren, *History of the Ojibwa Nation* (Minneapolis: Ross and Haines, 1957); N. H. Winchell, *The Aborgines of Minnesota* (St. Paul: Minnesota Historical Society, 1911).

The following notes include our interpretation of the Midewiwin, based on the published sources listed in the preceding paragraph and from information told to us by old Ojibwa.

Entrance into the society.

The Ojibwa considered the ceremonies of the Mide society sacred in character. Entrance was an extremely serious undertaking. Requirements were severe and preparation often extended over a period of several years. There were conferences with leaders who gave instructions to the candidate in medicine, myths, songs, and magic. There were also requirements of fasts, and purifications through sweat baths. The fees, which were to be paid in blankets, pelts, kettles, guns, and other useful gifts, were hard to meet, and therefore many people were prohibited from entering more than one or two of the four or eight degrees. Gifts of tobacco were always mandatory at all instructions and meetings.

Mide lodge.

The ceremonies of the Midewiwin took place in a special kind of wigwam or lodge called the Midewigan. The framework of poles and saplings stood from year to year, and some of them remain to this day. Since the ceremony usually occurred in late spring or summer, only the lower part of the structure was enclosed. It was covered by green branches loosely interwoven. The lodge was planned so that the length of the structure should lie east and west. Since the east was significant in the Mide myths, it was definitely prescribed that the main entrance should be located on that side.

Objects used in the ceremony.

Within the Mide lodge, just beyond the entrance, was a large *stone* lying on the ground. The early Ojibwa considered this stone sacred, as they did other objects used in the ceremony.

Farther inside the Midewigan was the sacred *post* about five to seven feet in height. For each successive degree, another post was added, each being painted with symbolic colors. In the fourth degree, the post added to the previous

115

three had a cross-beam fitted into it. It was this cross which Father Hennepin and Father Marquette, missionaries of the seventeenth century, came upon in their travels, and naturally they thought it was a symbol of the Christian religion. One of our informants said that the candidiate provided his own post for each degree and that he could afterward erect it before his lodge, or in some other place. At the death of the member, the post was placed over the grave.

In addition to the stone and the posts, there were only a few other objects used in this important religious ceremony. Two of these, the drum and the rattle, were instruments for accompanying the chant and the dance.

The *drum* (called mitiquakik) differed from the usual dance drum in that it was constructed according to definite regulations. Barrel-like in shape, it was hollowed out by hand from a tree trunk. Water was placed in a special compartment in the bottom of the drum, and deer hide of a certain age was stretched tightly over the top and bottom. Into the side, a small hole was bored and then plugged in order to keep the water level the same. This was done so that the tone would not fluctuate. Only certain ritually defined designs could be used to decorate the drum. Some of these seen in our research were the star, moon, sun, thunderbird, heart, hand, medicine man's eye, bear paw, and the abode of the manidos. In beating the drum, the Ojibwa used hammer-like sticks with the end carved to represent heads of birds and animals important in the rites. All of the symbols relating to the drum and sticks were carefully explained by the Mide priest (or leader) to his pupil. The priest also explained

116

that the mitiquakik was the gift of Kijie manido through Nanabozho and that it was used to invoke the good manidos and to expel the evil ones hovering outside and within the Midewigan. Kijie manido was depicted on some of the scrolls as playing the drum.

The ceremonial rattles were made by hollowing gourds and partially filling them with seeds or pebbles. Like the drum, the rattles were decorated with symbolic designs, such as the four winds, the hand, and the heart.

An exceedingly important object which every member of the Midewiwin owned was a *medicine sack* (pinjigusan) made of the complete skin of prescribed animals. The kind of animal used for the sack represented the degree attained. It was virtually a certificate of the owner's knowledge of plants to be used for protective medicine and for magic. In it, the members of the Midewiwin carried medicinal herbs and the white migis shell, the main emblem of the society. The medicine sack was so revered that it was never displayed without a definite ceremony, and it was buried with the owner at death.

The *ceremonial pipe* (adopwagan) was usually made of wood or limestone, red or black sandstone, black shale or black slate. As in other objects associated with the Midewiwin, ritualistic designs were used.

Myths relate how Nanabozho gave *tobacco* (opakosigan) to the Ojibwa and how he taught them to use it in appeasing the manidos by leaving some tobacco as a gift or by making a smoke offering. In the Mide ceremonies, as well as in all festive occasions, smoking played an important role. This was the usual ritual: The Ojibwa first pointed the stem to the east and then he repeated the ceremony for each of the other directions, continuing the clockwise order south, west, and north. Then he pointed the stem upward to the sky and after that, downward to the earth and the home of the dead.

The objects mentioned so far were all part of the rites within the lodge. As the time for the ceremony drew near, a messenger was sent out with a definite number of small painted *sticks* which virtually served as tickets of admission to the meeting. The invited members assembled and erected wigwams in the area of the Mide lodge.

In our research we found that among other traditions, the sacred *number four* (or a multiple of four) was emphasized in several ways. A few of these are:

four officiating priests
four degrees (or eight)
four encirclements of the lodge outside and inside
four purification ceremonies in the sweat lodge
four directions in a clockwise order beginning with the east
   Scrolls

The birchbark *scrolls,* or charts, owned by the priests of the Mide society, were made of rolls of birch bark fastened together by narrow strips of wood. Some of the delineations on the charts were easily identified, but the arrangement and sequence of these figures made the reading of the scrolls impossible save to one who had been instructed in their interpretation. Even in the days when the authority of the Midewiwin was at its height, only those few who had attained the final degrees of the organization understood the full significance of what was pictured.

In 1933 Charlie Fox, a leader of the Mide ceremonies at Naytahwaush on the White Earth Reservation, gave permission to Sister Bernard Coleman to photograph a scroll used there in the Midewiwin by him and by his father, White Fox.

At the extreme left are pictured the four corners of the earth. Bear paws represent the steps which the initiate should follow in the ceremonies. Underwater serpents and other evil manidos are portrayed as obstacles in the candidate's path from one degree to the next. (Animal manidos emphasized on the Mide chart were the serpent, panther, lynx, bear, turtle, and otter. Birds were also given prominence. Thunderbirds, or animikig, were represented by eagles, hawks, or other awe-inspiring birds. Some of the animals were considered helpful and some were not.)

On the Naytahwaush chart a wavy line, symbolizing spirit power, appears around a human figure. Natural phenomena such as trees are etched on the chart, and also wigwams or lodges which designate the number of feasts given for the leader by the initiate. These feasts were given as recompense for the lessons. Other pictorial representations are more formalized and therefore less evident. A concept commonly portrayed on these charts is the path of life and the many tangents which divert the individual.

Songs

Songs were important in the ritual of the Mide society. A new member could claim those sung during his initiation if he could remember them. However, it was not only in the Midewiwin that songs were important. They entered into practically all Ojibwa activities—war, hunting, ricing, and social festivities. Rights to songs were acquired through dreams or through purchase. Nanabozho was often the subject of Ojibwa songs.

119

Myths of the Mide ceremony.

Myths and legendary history were interwoven throughout the ritual of the Mide ceremonies. The Ojibwa were told the circumstances under which Nanabozho transmitted the mystic rite to the Indians through the help of the otter. They were also taught the legendary history of the westward migration of the An-ish-in-aub-ag, or the early people. A summary of one of these accounts follows:

Nanabozho looks down from his home above and observes the distress of the An-ish-in-aub-ag, who inhabit the four corners of the earth. He wishes to help them. He sees an otter who appears in the water to the west. The otter disappears and then it appears in the north, then the east, south and finally again to the west. Then he comes to the center of the earth. Then Nanabozho descends to the earth and instructs the otter in the Mide religion. He teaches him the songs and gives him the articles to use in the ceremonies. He confers upon him the medicine sack and shoots into his body the sacred migis (a white shell, the emblem of life).

After receiving the mystic rite, the otter teaches the ceremony to the An-ish-in-aub-ag. The early people migrate from the east westward to Sault Ste. Marie, to La Pointe, and finally to Minnesota. Wherever the otter stops, a Mide lodge is set up, and life is given to the people. Thus the path of the otter is the path of life.[1]

---

[1] During 1887-89 W. J. Hoffman made a study of the Mide religion as practiced on northern Minnesota reservations. This myth is based on a Mide leader's interpretation of a birchbark chart. See W. J. Hoffman, "The Midewiwin, or 'Grand Medicine Society' of the Ojibwa," in **Seventh Annual Report of the Bureau of Ethnology,** Washington, D. C.: Government Printing Office, 1891, 175-80.

A variation in the myth just summarized is the substitution of the migis shell for the otter: Wherever the migis shell appears above the water, the rays of the sun reflect from its glossy back and it gives light and life to the An-ish-in-aub-ag.[2]

Other myths associated with the bestowal of the Mide rites concentrate on the restoring of an Ojibwa boy to life through the East manido[3] or else through the Sun manido. In the latter myth the Sun manido calls upon the bear to transmit life to the boy.[4] The bear bestows spirit power upon the boy by blowing upon his medicine sack.

In all of the myths mentioned so far, the central theme is the giving of life through the transmission of spirit power. The reenactment of this theme was the climax of the Mide ceremony when a candidate was initiated into the society. By means of the "shooting" or pointing of the medicine sack (an animal skin), and particularly the migis shell, spirit power was given to the initiate. The renewal of spirit power by each member pointing his medicine sack containing his migis shell toward his neighbor was an important tradition of the society and served as a strong bond of unity which did not otherwise exist among the Ojibwa.

Other mythological themes in the Mide ceremony include the conflict between Nanabozho and the evil under-

---

[2] William Warren, **History of the Ojibway Nation,** (Minneapolis: Ross and Haines, 1957), 78-81.

---

[3] Frances Densmore, **Chippewa Music,** Bureau of American Ethnology, Bulletin 45 (Washington, D. C.: Government Printing Office), 21-23.

---

[4] W. J. Hoffman, **op. cit.,** 172-173.

water manidos (panther, lion, lynx, snake) and the eventual formation of the new earth for the Ojibwa. In the ritual of the Midewiwin the candidate for each degree had to meet the opposition of the evil animal manidos that tried to prevent him from making progress in the society. Good animal manidos helped the candidate to advance.

To instruct those who wished to become members of the society, and to perform the long ceremonies, the leaders needed the help of symbolic designs. Otherwise they would have to depend entirely on memory. A system of such designs was developed almost to the point of true hieroglyphics or picture writing. Possible codification beyond this stage was interrupted by the coming of the white man, but the designs themselves, etched on birch-bark charts or scrolls, helped to some extent to preserve the traditions of the society. These symbolic designs were arranged according to a sequence of ideas that could be interpreted only by a person educated in the teachings of the Midewiwin. Naturally, with the passage of time and the separation of people, variations appeared in both the symbolism and the interpretation. In general, it seems to be true that the traditions of the society became more elaborate as time went along.

BIBLIOGRAPHY

Part I. The Minnesota Ojibwa

Comparatively few records have been made of the folk literature of the Minnesota Ojibwa. An early source is to be found in a report by McKenney, who in 1827 included an important episode from Ojibwa mythology in his comments on a visit at Fond du Lac, Minnesota. (10) Another early account appeared in 1830. In an autobiographical narrative, Tanner, a white man who lived part of his life among the Ojibwa of northwestern Minnesota, revealed the role of mythology in the everyday life of the Indian. (13) The year 1885 marked the publication of Warren's history, which included legendary material concerning the early migrations, the various clans, and religious rituals. (14) The history is of particular interest since the writer himself was an Ojibwa.

Toward the end of the nineteenth century, W. J. Hoffman was sent by the Bureau of American Ethnology to northern Minnesota to gather information about the Ojibwa Midewiwin or the Grand Medicine Society. (8) A significant part of Hoffman's report contained native mythology.

During the years 1903-05, William Jones conducted research that had for its specific purpose the recording of Ojibwa myths and tales. (9) His narrators in northern Minnesota were Bois Fort and Leech Lake Ojibwa. (There were also some from the Fort William-Lake Nipigon region in Canada.) The fruit of the work is to be found in the two volumes of Ojibwa *Texts,* published by the Ameri-

123

can Ethnological Society in 1917 and 1919 under the editorship of Truman Michelson. The stories appear in both the native language and in the literal translation, with no phrasing into more idiomatic English. In singleness of purpose and in comprehensiveness of content, the collection by Jones is outstanding in the records of Minnesota Ojibwa folk literature.

Frances Densmore was another research worker on northern Minnesota reservations at the beginning of the twentieth century. (5) (6) Her studies were sponsored by the Bureau of American Ethnology. While her main interest was in music and not in folk literature, she included a few myths and other stories in her reports.

A year after the publication of Densmore's *Chippewa Music* in 1910, a European by the name of de Josselin de Jong, conservator at the State Museum of Ethnography in Leiden, came to the Red Lake Reservation to learn more about the Ojibwa language. (4) The myths that he recorded, although incidental to his main purpose, are an important part of the Minnesota collection.

Sister Bernard Coleman's research into the decorative designs of Minnesota Ojibwa was based on material gathered on reservations during the years 1929-45. (2) The designs that are explained and illustrated in the study often express concepts found in Ojibwa mythology.

Some stories from northern Minnesota reservations have been reported in the *Journal of American Folklore* (designated in the bibliography as JAFL). In 1928, Reagan published tales that he had recorded earlier at Nett Lake, and in 1911, Michelson made a brief report of narratives from White Earth. (12) (11)

Most of the sources commented on include information about the background and customs of the Minnesota Ojibwa. Other references that contribute here are (1), (3), (7), and (15).

1. Brown, Paula, "Changes in Ojibwa Social Control," *American Anthropologist,* January, 1952, pp. 57 ff.

2. Coleman, Sister Bernard, *Decorative Designs of the Ojibwa of Northern Minnesota,* Catholic University of America Press, 1947.

3. Coleman, Sister Bernard, "The Religion of the Ojibwa of Northern Minnesota," *Primitive Man,* July and October, 1937, pp. 1 ff.

4. de Josselin de Jong, J. P. B., "Original Odzibwe-Texts" in *Baessler Archiv.* 5:1-54, Leipzig and Berlin, 1913.

5. Densmore, Frances, *Chippewa Customs,* Bureau of American Ethnology Bulletin 86, Government Printing Office, 1929.

6. Densmore, Frances, *Chippewa Music,* Bureau of American Ethnology Bulletin 45, Government Printing Office, 1910.

7. Gilfillan, Joseph A., "The Ojibways in Minnesota," *Minnesota Historical Society Collections,* 1901, pp. 55 ff.

8. Hoffman, W. J., "The Midewiwin or 'Grand Medicine Society' of the Ojibwa," in *Seventh Annual Report of the Bureau of American Ethnology,* pp. 149-300, Government Printing Office, 1891.

9. Jones, William (ed. by Truman Michelson), *Ojibwa Texts,* Publications of the American Ethnological So-

ciety, Vol. 7; Part 1, E. J. Brill, 1917, and Part 2, Arbor Press, 1919.

10. McKenney, Thomas, *Sketches of a Tour of the Lakes,* Fielding Lucas, 1827.

11. Michelson, Truman, "Ojibwa Tales," JAFL, April-June, 1911, pp. 249 ff.

12. Radin, Paul and Reagan, A. B., "Ojibwa Myths and Tales," JAFL, January-March, 1928, pp. 61 ff.

13. Tanner, John, *A Narrative of the Captivity and Adventures of John Tanner During Thirty Years Residence Among the Indians in the Interior of North America* (1830), Ross and Haines, Inc., 1956.

14. Warren, William W., *History of the Ojibway Nation,* Ross and Haines, Inc., 1957. (See also *Minnesota Historical Society Collections,* 1885, pp. 21 ff.)

15. Winchell, N. H., *et al, The Aborigines of Minnesota,* Minnesota Historical Society, 1911.

Part II. Related References

Part II of the bibliography contains general references on folk literature and Indian narratives. It also includes additional references to particular sources that lend interest and significance to the stories that we collected at the end of the 1950's.

1. Boas, Franz, "Dissemination of Tales Among the Natives of North America," JAFL, January-March, 1891, pp. 13 ff.

2. Boas, Franz, *Race, Language and Culture,* Macmillan Company, 1940.

3. Carson, William, "Ojibwa Tales," JAFL, July-September, 1917, pp. 491 ff.

4. Chamberlain, A. F., "Nanibozhu A m o n g s t the Otchipwe, Mississagas, and Other Algonkian Tribes," JAFL, July-September, 1891, pp. 193 ff.

5. Cox, Marian Roalfe, *Cinderella,* Publications of the Folk-Lore Society, London, 1893.

6. Davidson, D. S., "Folk Tales from Grand Lake Victoria, Quebec," JAFL, April-June, 1928, pp. 275 ff.

7. Davidson, D. S., "Tete-de-Boule Tales," JAFL, April-June, 1928, pp. 262 ff.

8. Davis, Rose M., "How Indian Is Hiawatha?", *Midwest Folklore,* Spring, 1957, pp. 5 ff.

9. Delarue, Paul (ed.), *The Borzoi Book of French Folk Tales,* Alfred A. Knopf, 1956.

10. Dorson, Richard M., *Bloodstoppers and Bearwalkers,* Harvard University Press, 1952.

11. Elder, William, "The Aborigines of Nova Scotia," *North American Review,* January, 1871, pp. 1 ff.

12. Fisher, Margaret W., "The Mythology of the Northern and Northeastern Algonkians in Reference to Algonkian Mythology as a Whole," in Frederick Johnson (ed.), *Man in Northeastern North America,* pp. 226-62, Peabody Foundation for Archaelogy, Andover, Massachusetts, 1946.

13. Hallowell, A. I., "Concordance of Ojibwa Narratives in the Published Works of Henry R. Schoolcraft," JAFL, April, 1946, pp. 136 ff.

14. Hallowell, A. I., *Culture and Experience,* University of Pennsylvania Press, 1955.

15. Hennepin, Father Louis, *A New Discovery of a Vast*

127

Country in America, Vol. 2 (1698) (ed. by Reuben Gold Thwaites), A. C. McClurg, 1903.

16. *The Jesuit Relations and Allied Documents: Travels and Explorations of the Jesuit Missionaries in New France, 1610-1791* (ed. by Reuben Gold Thwaites), Burrows Brothers, 1896-1901. (Volumes 5, 6, 10, 12, 15, 54, 57, 61, 65, and *passim*).

17. Jones, William, "The Algonkin Manitou," JAFL, July-September, 1905, pp. 183 ff.

18. Kinietz, W. Vernon, *Chippewa Village,* Cranbrook Institute of Science, 1947.

19. Kohl, J. G., *Kitchi-Gami: Wanderings Round Lake Superior* (1860), Ross and Haines, Inc., 1956.

20. Leach, Maria (ed.), *Dictionary of American Folklore, Mythology, and Legend,* Funk and Wagnalls Company, 1949, 1950, 2 vols.

21. Osborn, Chas S. and Osborn, Stellanova, *Schoolcraft-Longfellow-Hiawatha,* Jacques Cattell Press, 1942.

22. Radin, Paul, *The Trickster: A Study in American Indian Mythology,* Routledge and Kegan Paul, 1956.

23. Rooth, Anna Birgitta, "The Creation Myths of North American Indians," *Anthropos,* 1957, pp. 497 ff.

24. Schmerler, Henrietta, "Trickster Marries His Daughter," JAFL, April-June, 1931, pp. 196 ff.

25. Skinner, Alanson, "Bungi Tales," JAFL, January-March, 1928, pp. 159 ff.

26. Skinner, Alanson, "Plains Ojibwa Tales," JAFL, April- June, 1919, pp. 280 ff.

27. Speck, Frank G., "Montagnais and Naskapi Tales from t h e Labrador Peninsula," JAFL, January-March, 1925, pp. 1 ff.

28. Squier, E. G., "Manabozho and the Great Serpent," *American Review,* Part 2, October, 1848, pp. 395 ff.
29. Stamp, Harley, "The Water-Fairies," JAFL, July-September, 1915, pp. 310 ff.
30. Thompson, Stith, *The Folktale,* Dryden Press, 1946.
31. Thompson, Stith, "The Indian Legend of Hiawatha," *Publications of the Modern Language Association,* March, 1922, pp. 128 ff.
32. Thompson, Stith, *Tales of the North American Indians,* Harvard University Press, 1929.
33. Williams, Mentor L. (ed.) *Schoolcraft's I n d i a n Legends,* Michigan State University Press, 1956.

INDEX

Adultery, attitude toward, 46
Agriculture, 6-7
Ah-che-dah-mo, 96
Algonquian Indians, 4, 55, 59
Animals
  Great or giant animals, 5, 56-57, 69
  Stories, 37-44, 62-65, 70-72, 74-82
  (See also Dodem, Hunting lore, Manido)
Animikig, see Thunderbird
An-ish-in-aub-ag, 4
  Mystic rite, 120
Antidote, 14, 111

Bags, 102, 111
  Mide medicine sack, 117
Barter, 6
Baskets, 83
Battles
  Iroquois, 4
  Leech Lake Uprising, 3
  Sioux, 3
Birch bark, uses of, 83, 91
Birds, 105
  Chickadee, 104-106
  Crow, 3
  Oriole, 36, 38
  Owl, 36, 39
  Robin, 36-38
Blood-boy, story of, 45
Bones, regurgitation of, 107

Bonga, Jean, 23
Brown, 125
Bull roarer, 106
Bunyan, Paul, 97
  Story, 99
Burial customs, 91-92
Buzzer, see Bull roarer

Cardinal directions, 56, 61, 102, 106, 118
Cass Lake, 14, 98, 103
Cedar, 91
Ceremonies, initiation into Midewiwin, 114, 120-122
Charms, 106-107, 109-112
Children
  Charms, 106, 110
  Games and play, 106
  Fasting, 37
  Naming, 103
  Story telling, 5-6, 8, 36, 39, 101
  (See also Family, Schools)
Coleman, 114, 119, 124, 125
Copper, 43
Courtship tests, 12, 42-43
Creation of the world, 60
Culture hero, Nanabozho as, 5, 58, 60, 62, 86, 97

Death, accounted for, 61
Deer, uses of, 12, 98
de Josslin de Jong, 92, 124, 125

133